GALATIANS

$\mathscr{F}ree$
in Christ

A Guided Discovery for Groups and Individuals

Kevin Perrotta

LOYOLAPRESS.

CHICAGO

LOYOLA PRESS.
A JESUIT MINISTRY

3441 N. Ashland Avenue
Chicago, Illinois 60657
(800) 621-1008
www.loyolapress.com

Nihil Obstat
Reverend Peter Damian Akpunono, S.T.D., S.S.L.
Censor Deputatus
November 19, 2003

Imprimatur
Most Reverend Edwin M. Conway, D.D.
Vicar General
Archdiocese of Chicago
December 4, 2003

The *Nihil Obstat* and *Imprimatur* are official declarations that a book is free of doctrinal and moral error. No implication is contained therein that those who have granted the *Nihil Obstat* and *Imprimatur* agree with the content, opinions, or statements expressed. Nor do they assume any legal responsibility associated with publication.

Unless otherwise noted, the Scripture quotations contained herein are from the New Revised Standard Version Bible: Catholic Edition, copyright © 1993 and 1989 by the Division of Christian Education of the National Council of the Churches of Christ in the U.S.A. Used by permission. All rights reserved. Subheadings in Scripture quotations have been added by Kevin Perrotta.

The excerpts from the letters of St. Catherine of Siena (p. 37) are from Suzanne Noffke, O.P., trans., *The Letters of Catherine of Siena*, vol. 2, Medieval and Renaissance Texts and Studies, vol. 203 (Tempe, Ariz.: Arizona Center for Medieval and Renaissance Studies, 2001), 21, 63.

The "Saints in the Making" on St. John Gabriel Perboyre (p. 53) is written by Bert Ghezzi and is adapted from an article that originally appeared in *God's Word Today*, September 2003.

The excerpt from a letter of Blessed Columba Marmion (p. 67) is taken from Raymond Thibaut, trans. and ed., *Union with God according to the Letters of Direction of Dom Marmion* (St. Louis, Mo.: B. Herder Book Co., 1934).

The excerpt from a letter of J. Hudson Taylor (p. 81) is from Dr. and Mrs. Howard Taylor, *Hudson Taylor's Spiritual Secret* (London: China Inland Mission, 1932). More information about Taylor may be found in Howard Taylor, *Hudson Taylor and the China Inland Mission: The Growth of a Work of God* (Philadelphia: The China Inland Mission, 1918).

More information about Satoko Kitahara (p. 91) may be found in Ann Ball, *Faces of Holiness II* (Huntington, Ind.: Our Sunday Visitor, 2001), and Boniface Hanley, O.F.M., *With Minds of Their Own* (Notre Dame, Ind.: Ave Maria Press, 1991).

Interior design by Kay Hartmann/Communique Design
Illustration by Charise Mericle Harper

ISBN-13: 978-0-8294-2007-4
ISBN-10: 0-8294-2007-X

Printed in the United States of America
14 15 16 17 18 19 20 Bang 10 9 8 7 6 5 4 3 2

Contents

How to Use This Guide

You might compare the Bible to a national park. The park is so large that you could spend months, even years, getting to know it. But a brief visit, if carefully planned, can be enjoyable and worthwhile. In a few hours you can drive through the park and pull over at a handful of sites. At each stop you can get out of the car, take a short trail through the woods, listen to the wind blowing through the trees, get a feel for the place.

In this booklet, we will read Paul's letter to the Galatians. Because the letter is fairly short, we will be able to read almost all of it in six sessions. The excerpts also are not very long, and so we will be able to walk through them at a leisurely pace, thinking carefully about what we are reading and what it means for our lives today.

This guide provides everything you need to explore Galatians in six discussions—or to do a six-part exploration on your own. The introduction on page 6 will prepare you to get the most out of your reading. The weekly sections provide explanations that will help illuminate the meanings of the readings of Paul's letter for your life. Equally important, each section supplies questions that will launch your group into fruitful discussion, helping you to both investigate Galatians for yourself and learn from one another. If you're using the booklet by yourself, the questions will spur your personal reflection.

Each discussion is meant to be a *guided discovery.*

Guided. None of us is equipped to read the Bible without help. We read the Bible *for* ourselves but not *by* ourselves. Scripture was written to be understood and applied in the community of faith. So each week "A Guide to the Reading," drawing on the work of both modern biblical scholars and Christian writers of the past, supplies background and explanations. The guide will help you grasp the meanings of Galatians. Think of it as a friendly park ranger who points out noteworthy details and explains what you're looking at so you can appreciate things for yourself.

Discovery. The purpose is for *you* to interact with Paul's letter to the Galatians. "Questions for Careful Reading" is a tool to help you dig into the text and examine it carefully. "Questions for Application" will help you consider what these words mean for your life here and now. Each week concludes with an "Approach to

Prayer" section that helps you respond to God's word. Supplementary "Living Tradition" and "Saints in the Making" sections offer the thoughts and experiences of Christians past and present. By showing what Paul's themes of Galatians have meant to others, these sections will help you consider what they mean for you.

How long are the discussion sessions? We've assumed you will have about an hour and a half when you get together. If you have less time, you'll find that most of the elements can be shortened somewhat.

Is homework necessary? Yes. Some background information and a few key explanations are crucial for grasping the meaning of Paul's letter to the Galatians. This guide will provide you with a helpful minimum of such assistance. You can expect to have fruitful discussions if you read the weekly explanatory material and prepare answers to the questions in advance of each meeting. The "Guides to the Reading" in Weeks 2–5 are longer than in other Six Weeks with the Bible books, in order to give you extra help to penetrate the meaning of this sometimes difficult letter.

What about leadership? If you happen to have a world-class biblical scholar in your group, by all means ask him or her to lead the discussions. In the absence of any professional Scripture scholars, or even accomplished amateur biblical scholars, you can still have a first-class Bible discussion. Choose two or three people to take turns as facilitators, and have everyone read "Suggestions for Bible Discussion Groups" (page 92) before beginning.

Does everyone need a guide? a Bible? Everyone in the group will need his or her own copy of this booklet. It contains all the text of Galatians discussed in the weekly sessions, so a Bible is not absolutely necessary—but each participant will find it useful to have one. And one or two of the questions do involve looking at other passages in the Bible that are not contained in this guide. You should have at least one Bible on hand for your discussions (see page 96 for recommendations.)

How do we get started? Before you begin, take a look at the suggestions for Bible discussion groups (page 92) or individuals (page 95).

Extreme Bible Reading

Like athletic activities that span a range of intensity, the books of the New Testament make various demands on our concentration. At one end of the range, the little books such as 2 and 3 John are a walk in the park. Most of the books are more challenging. The letter of James is a vigorous tennis match, the Gospel of John is eighteen holes of golf on a championship course. At the far end of the range are the extreme sports: Hebrews (snowboarding?), Revelation (rock climbing?)—and Galatians. Galatians is a gut wrencher, the swimming-biking-running triathlon of the New Testament, all packed into six chapters.

Without preliminaries, at verse 1 of Galatians we plunge immediately into a fast-flowing narrative. Farther on, as we emerge onto the dry land of theological discussion, the course leads steeply upward, through towering issues of literally cosmic importance. Passing through a theological battlefield, we feel the bruising impact of the most severe doctrinal crisis the Church has ever faced—the conflict that almost tore the young Church apart. As we speed through arguments based on Old Testament texts, we must stay alert to avoid treacherous quicksands of terminology and to keep from being overwhelmed by disputes that have raged in the Christian world ever since the Reformation. If we persevere and reach our goal, we will arrive at the point where St. Paul stands and will be able to look out with him as he views God's decisive action in the world through his Son and his Holy Spirit— and we will see what God's action means for us.

Are you *ready* for this?

As we gear up to read Galatians, we must prepare for a crucial challenge. In his letter to the Galatians, Paul focuses on a problem that we no longer face. Thank God, it was laid to rest long ago, partly through Paul's efforts. Thus, reading Galatians means going back into the past and witnessing a dispute over a dead issue in order to find a living message for ourselves today.

There are two dangers here. First, if we do not understand the problem that Paul was dealing with, we may misunderstand his words and read a different meaning into them. The result? We miss the message that Paul has for us. The second danger is that we may get lost in exploring the complex first-century situation that

Paul faced and never make it back to the twenty-first century with the meaning of his message for ourselves.

Let's avoid both these dangers! To do so, we will look here at the problem Paul dealt with in Galatia and preview the value of his letter for us today. This will take a few pages, but stay with me. We're getting in shape for the main event.

To begin, let's go back to the beginning of Christianity, to Jesus, and consider an item of crucial importance. Jesus was a Jew.

God had chosen the Jews for a special relationship with himself. Through Moses, God made a covenant with the Jews (at the time, they were called Israelites, but *Jews* was the common name by the first century). He gave the Jews instructions for a holy way of life. This "Law of Moses" (considered to be the first five books of the Bible) contained the Ten Commandments, which expressed fundamental moral principles. "Thou shalt not kill," for example, enshrined the inviolability of innocent human life (Exodus 20:13—King James Version). But the Law also contained much more, such as

- ◆ a cycle of festivals that acknowledged that land and fertility are gifts from God and recalled God's saving deeds (Deuteronomy 16)
- ◆ a pattern of animal sacrifice that expressed thanks to God and atoned for sins (Leviticus 1–7)
- ◆ a symbolic ceremonial system—including regulations about clean and unclean foods, definitions of clean and unclean activities, ritual means of restoring cleanness—all of which reflected the people's awareness of God's holy presence among them (Leviticus 11–15)

The Mosaic Law, in other words, comprised an entire way of life.

While Jews and non-Jews (gentiles) shared many convictions about the nature of the divine and the right way for humans to live, the Mosaic Law created a distinction between them. The Mosaic Law produced a way of life that was distinct from the cultures of surrounding peoples because it was based on somewhat different beliefs about God and morality.

Certain aspects of the Mosaic Law became boundary markers between Jews and gentiles. For example, the Mosaic regulations about circumcising male children, abstaining from ceremonially unclean foods, and ceasing from work on the Sabbath expressed Jews' consciousness of being in a special relationship with God and made them visibly different from their gentile neighbors. These rules had taken on particular importance as tokens of Jews' faithfulness to God during the couple of centuries before Jesus, when persecutors tried to force Jews to abandon them. Expressing their loyalty to God, Jews suffered persecution, even death, for circumcising their boys and refusing to eat food unacceptable under the Mosaic Law (2 Maccabees 6:18–7:41; Tobit 1:10–13; Judith 10:5; 12:1–20; Esther 14:17; Daniel 1:8–16).

In addition to giving them a Law, God led the Jewish people to hope that he was going to carry out a world-changing, life-giving plan on their behalf. During his ministry, Jesus presented himself as the supreme agent of this climactic divine action. Jesus indicated that through his death and resurrection he would reconcile human beings with God (Luke 22:19–20). He would provide the life-giving blessing of God's presence and the power to live a holy life (John 6; 35–58).

Jesus presented himself and his promise of life to his fellow Jews. Inevitably the question arose for the early Church: What significance did Jesus have for the non-Jewish world? Would gentiles who came to believe in Jesus have to buy into the whole religious and cultural package laid out in the Mosaic Law? Would they step across the chasm marked out by the Mosaic Law between gentiles and Jews and join the Jewish people?

Jesus himself did not answer this question. He directed his earthly ministry to fellow Jews (Mark 7:24–29). He limited his disciples' training missions to Jewish recipients (Matthew 10:5–6). Jesus did treat gentiles with a warmth and appreciation that suggested his ministry held great significance for them, too (Matthew 8:5–13). But only after his resurrection did he commission his followers to make him known not only to Jews but to all other peoples as well. As to how the gentiles who believed in him should relate to the Jewish people, Jesus left it up to his followers to discover as they carried out their mission. They would have the Spirit's guidance in their ministry and could observe the results of the Spirit's activity. By reflecting on these events, as well as by reading Scripture in light of Jesus' life and teaching, they would learn what they needed to know. Jesus had a remarkable confidence in the power of the Holy Spirit—and a remarkable confidence in the ability of his followers, as a community, to perceive his intentions after his departure from them.

At first, Jesus' followers seem to have operated on the basis of unexamined assumptions. The Jews are God's people; the Mosaic Law expresses his will for us; our Messiah has now come, bringing the ultimate interpretation of this Law and giving us the power to follow it according to God's original intentions. Why wouldn't gentiles who are attracted to Jesus embrace this Law and join us, his people? But soon the Holy Spirit began to shake this assumption.

The Spirit directed Peter, the leader of Jesus' inner group of followers, to visit a gentile named Cornelius and tell him and his friends about Jesus. When Peter did this, Cornelius and company believed in Jesus and very demonstrably received the Holy Spirit. Peter was astonished to see that these gentiles had in effect become Christians without becoming Jews. Peter baptized Cornelius and his friends, sealing their membership in the Church (Acts 10). Were they also obliged to follow the Mosaic Law? In the minds of many Jewish Christians, the answer was probably "of course." But further action of the Holy Spirit soon introduced a whole new way of looking at the question.

On his way from Jerusalem to persecute Jewish Christians in Damascus, a Jewish leader named Saul received an overpowering vision of Jesus (Acts 9) and felt himself called to preach Jesus to gentiles (1:16—unless noted, all biblical citations in this book refer to Galatians). Before this, Saul—better known as Paul—had been very devoted to the Mosaic Law. He was a Pharisee, a group of Jews who attempted to keep the Law rigorously and pro-moted rigorous observance by other Jews (Philippians 3:4–6). Now Paul realized that God had moved his interaction with the human race into a new—and final—phase, in which he was himself accessible to

9

all people *directly* through his Son, apart from his covenant with the Jewish people. Thus Paul felt it was unnecessary for gentile believers in Jesus to become Jews and keep all of the Mosaic Law.

Paul began to operate on the basis of this understanding of God's action in the world. He set off to do missionary work among Arabs in an area corresponding to present-day Jordan and southern Syria (1:15–17). For years he labored far from Jerusalem, feeling no need to consult the leadership of the community there. Later, with a base of operations in Antioch (then a large city, today a town in Turkey), Paul evangelized gentiles in what is now Turkey and Greece without requiring them to become Jews.

But while Paul happily went about building Law-free, gentile Christian communities, many Jewish Christians continued to think that keeping the Mosaic Law was essential for a full relationship with God. As Paul and like-minded missionaries brought an increasing number of gentiles into the Church, the irreconcilable differences between these approaches produced a crisis. Church leaders were forced to resolve the conflict one way or the other.

At a distance of twenty centuries, it is impossible to determine precisely how the Church's earliest leaders worked through the problem. Both Paul (2:1–10) and Luke (Acts 15) describe a pivotal meeting in Jerusalem, but their accounts do not match up perfectly. Apparently neither author has presented a complete record of the whole course of events. Paul's account is brief. Luke, following the practice of ancient historians, may have combined several incidents into a single episode in his account. Perhaps Jerusalem was the scene of more than one summit meeting.

In any case, at some point Christian leaders meeting in Jerusalem reached a momentous decision. They would not require gentile believers to be circumcised, that is, undertake to follow the whole Mosaic Law. These early Christian leaders were all Jews for whom their Jewish heritage was immensely important. To acknowledge that, through Christ, gentiles could relate to God without the Mosaic Law was a truly radical step for these men, undoubtedly achieved only with great inner struggle. But their process of radical self-examination was not yet over. For their answer to the question about gentile Christians and the Law opened up an even more radical question about Jewish Christians and the Law. If following the Mosaic Law is merely optional for gentile believers, why is it required for Jewish believers? Indeed, is it any longer required?

The agreement allowed that gentile believers do not have to follow the Mosaic Law. Do Jewish believers, then, follow it merely as a matter of cultural and religious heritage? Jesus has redeemed both Jews and gentiles. Does this mean that he has rendered the distinction between Jews and gentiles unimportant? What if observance of the Mosaic Law interferes with expressing the unity of Jew and gentile that Christ has accomplished: should Jewish believers then abandon these observances?

This last question took a very concrete form. Under what conditions should Jewish Christians eat with gentile Christians? The Lord's Supper and other festive meals, as well as meals of friendship, were an important feature of the Christians' community life. Inviting gentile believers to Jewish homes created no problem for the Jewish believers, because in their own homes they maintained the Mosaic dietary regulations. But could Jews eat in gentile believers' homes, where the food was not selected or prepared in a way that was acceptable under the Mosaic Law?

Should the Jewish Christians leave behind the dietary rules in the Law of Moses in order to express Christ's acceptance of the gentiles and his creation of a new community transcending the division of Jew and gentile? Or were they obliged to continue to observe the Mosaic Law, even though it produced a division in the Christian community?

A test case soon arose. Peter traveled to Antioch and, it seems, followed Paul's approach: he ate with gentiles in their homes, probably without inquiring too closely into what went into the casserole (setting a precedent followed, wisely or not, by generations of participants at church dinners). But then representatives arrived from James, who had succeeded Peter as the leader of the church in Jerusalem. Possibly they told Peter that his behavior was causing trouble for Jewish Christians back in Jerusalem. Other Jews were pointing to his behavior as evidence that the Christian movement led Jews to abandon the Mosaic Law. "While you are doing evangelistic and pastoral work in a mixed community," the representatives probably told Peter, "you should be careful to keep the Mosaic Law." Peter heeded this advice and stopped eating with the gentile believers.

Consider Peter's action from the point of view of a gentile Christian in Antioch. Imagine the revered leader of Jesus' disciples telling you that he cannot accept your invitation to dinner because your food is unclean. Might you also feel that he regards *you* as unclean, since you eat unclean food? The unspoken message in the refusal of Peter and the other Jewish believers to eat with you would be "you are not yet a full member of God's holy people." Jesus, you may conclude, is *not* all you need to be in full relationship with God. Without a word being said, you would feel pressured to embrace, in addition to Christ, the Mosaic Law.

Peter may not have thought through the consequences of his action. But Paul grasped what was at stake and rebuked Peter (2:11). How could anyone in the Church even imply that Christ is not all that is needed in order to be saved, Paul demanded indignantly.

Whether Paul carried the day in Antioch is unknown. Ultimately, the problem was resolved, perhaps by another meeting in Jerusalem. But as Paul writes to the Galatians, contradictory views of the issues involving Jews and gentiles are still competing in many of the church communities in the eastern Mediterranean.

And who were the Galatians? Galatia was a region in what today is central Turkey. Scholars have not reached agreement on the question of when Paul evangelized in Galatia. Whenever it was, after his departure other Jewish-Christian teachers came and presented the Galatians with a version of the gospel that differed considerably from Paul's. "You gentile believers," they declared, "need to complete your conversion by becoming Jews and following the Law of Moses."

Paul responds—we might even say he counterattacks— with the letter we are about to read. His argument is complex, but it boils down to this: "You gentile believers do not need to embrace the Mosaic Law," he insists, "because in Christ you already have everything that God offers." While many of us today admire Judaism and have great respect for Jewish religious life, very few of us are attracted by the idea of following the whole Mosaic Law or are worried that we might not be saved if we do not do so. But the reason that underlies Paul's assurance is as relevant to us now as it was two millennia ago: in Christ, God offers us everything that he can offer to human beings. Jesus is our point of access to all of God's grace, forgiveness, strength, wisdom, power, and joy.

Paul declares that Jesus is his life. He speaks of the Holy Spirit calling out "Father!" to God from within our hearts. To read Galatians with understanding is to move toward a deeper grasp of what Jesus means for us and of what it means to experience the transforming love of the Spirit that God places within us when we believe in Jesus. The Galatians were tempted to lose sight of Jesus and the Spirit within themselves. In our own way, so are we. Thus we need Paul's letter as much as the Galatians did.

The Galatians were being persuaded that the freedom from sin and the personal transformation they sought was unavailable to them outside the Mosaic Law. Paul's response was, simply, that only in the Spirit can we experience freedom and grow in love. In the face of our own discouragements at the pace of change in ourselves, our own confusions about the process of personal transformation, Paul's instruction about the work of the Spirit in us is as on target for us as it was for his Galatian converts.

As he argues against the appeal of the Mosaic Law for the gentile Galatian believers, Paul emphasizes over and over the priority of God's unconditional love, of God's initiative in the process of our salvation. In the midst of whatever distracts us from the presence of this initiative-taking God, of whatever causes us doubts about his gracious and unconditional love, Paul's message comes to us not as old words but as good news for today—which is precisely what Paul claims it is: the gospel, or good news, of Jesus Christ, the truth about God and his graciousness toward us.

In these ways, and others, Galatians will be a living word for us, if we make the effort to understand Paul's meaning and ponder his message for our lives.

Ready?

GETTING RIGHT TO THE POINT

Questions to Begin

15 minutes
Use a question or two to get warmed up for the reading.

---

1 What do you do now that you would not have predicted you would be doing ten years ago?

---

2 When have you made a decision that surprised your family?

Opening the Bible

5 minutes
*Read the passage aloud. Let individuals take turns reading
sections.*

The Reading: Galatians 1

Greetings, with a Prayer

1:1 Paul an apostle—sent neither by human commission nor from
human authorities, but through Jesus Christ and God the Father, who
raised him from the dead— 2 and all the members of God's family
who are with me,
To the churches of Galatia:
3 Grace to you and peace from God our Father and the Lord
Jesus Christ, 4 who gave himself for our sins to set us free from the
present evil age, according to the will of our God and Father, 5 to
whom be the glory forever and ever. Amen.

A Major Problem in Galatia

6 I am astonished that you are so quickly deserting the one who called
you in the grace of Christ and are turning to a different gospel— 7 not
that there is another gospel, but there are some who are confusing
you and want to pervert the gospel of Christ. 8 But even if we or an
angel from heaven should proclaim to you a gospel contrary to what
we proclaimed to you, let that one be accursed! 9 As we have said
before, so now I repeat, if anyone proclaims to you a gospel contrary
to what you received, let that one be accursed!
10 Am I now seeking human approval, or God's approval? Or
am I trying to please people? If I were still pleasing people, I would
not be a servant of Christ.

Where Paul Got His Message

11 For I want you to know, brothers and sisters, that the gospel that
was proclaimed by me is not of human origin; 12 for I did not receive
it from a human source, nor was I taught it, but I received it through
a revelation of Jesus Christ.
13 You have heard, no doubt, of my earlier life in Judaism. I
was violently persecuting the church of God and was trying to destroy
it. 14 I advanced in Judaism beyond many among my people of the
same age, for I was far more zealous for the traditions of my
ancestors. 15 But when God, who had set me apart before I was born
and called me through his grace, was pleased 16 to reveal his Son to

me, so that I might proclaim him among the Gentiles, I did not confer with any human being, 17 nor did I go up to Jerusalem to those who were already apostles before me, but I went away at once into Arabia, and afterwards I returned to Damascus.

18 Then after three years I did go up to Jerusalem to visit Cephas and stayed with him fifteen days; 19 but I did not see any other apostle except James the Lord's brother. 20 In what I am writing to you, before God, I do not lie!

21 Then I went into the regions of Syria and Cilicia, 22 and I was still unknown by sight to the churches of Judea that are in Christ; 23 they only heard it said, "The one who formerly was persecuting us is now proclaiming the faith he once tried to destroy." 24 And they glorified God because of me.

10 minutes
Choose questions according to your interest and time.

---

1 What word would you use to describe Paul's mood in 1:1–10?

---

2 Compare how Paul begins this letter to the way he opens his letters to the Christians in Philippi (Philippians 1:1–11) and Thessalonica (1 Thessalonians 1:1–10). What differences do you observe? What do they suggest about his attitude toward the Galatians?

---

3 How do you think the Galatians would have felt when this opening section of Paul's letter was read aloud at their community meeting?

---

4 In 1:1, 10, 11–12, and 18–20, Paul seems to be denying assertions that others have made about him. From these statements, what would you infer that others are saying about him?

A Guide to the Reading

If participants have not read this section already, read it aloud. Otherwise go on to "Questions for Application."

1:1–10. Paul opens some of his letters with warm expressions of confidence in the people to whom he writes. But not this letter. Paul is abrupt (1:6) and defensive (1:10, 20). He has no fond words for the Galatians. What's going on here?

A problem has arisen that Paul considers to be of the utmost importance. It concerns a twofold question: What has God done for humanity through Jesus' death and resurrection? And how should men and women respond to what God has done? Some other Christian teachers are giving the Galatians what Paul considers a distorted understanding of these issues. The Galatians do not seem to realize how serious the disagreement is. Accepting the other teachers' interpretation, Paul warns the Galatians, equals rejecting God (1:6).

The Galatian communities hang in the balance. They are in the process of "quickly deserting" God (1:6). Paul must act decisively to shore them up in their commitment to the truth. He speaks sharply to get their attention.

In this week's reading, Paul's reasoning is somewhat hard to follow because he begins to defend himself without clearly stating his position. Only at the end of next week's reading does he get to the point of declaring his interpretation of the gospel (2:16) and then showing why it is correct (2:17–4:31; in our readings in weeks 3 and 4).

From Paul's defensive statements we can make a guess at what the other teachers are saying about him. "He made a good start as a Christian missionary," they admit, "learning about Jesus from the twelve apostles in Jerusalem, then being sent out by the church in Antioch (Acts 12:25–13:3). But now he has abandoned the gospel as it was taught to him. He is trying to please people rather than God. In an effort to persuade people to follow Jesus, he is reducing the requirements of discipleship, giving them permission to follow Jesus without keeping the Law of Moses. That's neither what he learned in Jerusalem nor what he was commissioned to preach in Antioch. Paul has become a rogue apostle, marketing a fake version of the gospel. Don't listen to him!" These teachers probably claim to represent the Twelve in

Jerusalem and the church in Antioch, but there is reason to question whether they had such authorization.

In the face of these accusations, Paul insists immediately (1:1!) that he was *not* commissioned by any individual or group. He did not receive the gospel from other people, but from God, directly by a revelation of Jesus. Since no human being handed on the gospel to him, no human being is in a position to sit in judgment on his preaching. Since Jesus commissioned him, no one besides Jesus has the authority to decommission him. The Galatians should stick with him and his version of the gospel.

1:11–24. Paul carefully chooses the details in his account of his conversion and subsequent activities to support these points:

♦ The personal revelation of Jesus that was granted to him included "the gospel" that he now preaches (1:11–12; see Acts 9:3–22; 26:12–18).

♦ The zeal of his earlier life in Judaism (1:13–14) supports his contention that his Law-free gospel comes directly from God: who but God himself could have persuaded a person so committed to the Mosaic Law to trade it for anything else?

♦ The fact that he began to preach the gospel without consulting the apostles in Jerusalem (1:16–17) demonstrates that God gave him such a clear grasp of the gospel that he didn't need anyone to explain it to him.

♦ The astonishment of the Christian communities in Judea at his conversion (1:23–24) underlines the fact that only the intervention of God could account for the reversal in his life— and thus his version of the gospel also comes from God.

Perhaps because the other teachers claim that Paul has violated his commission from the Twelve in Jerusalem, Paul goes out of his way to demonstrate that he never had a close working relationship with the Twelve. He acknowledges that he made one trip to see Peter (Paul refers to him by the Aramaic form of his name— "Cephas"—rather than the Greek form—Peter; both forms mean "rock"). But it was a private visit (1:18–19), not an occasion for getting official authorization. Probably Paul used the visit to enlarge his fund of knowledge about Jesus' earthly life. After this, Paul went far away from the Twelve and had nothing to do with them (1:21–22).

Questions for Application

40 minutes
Choose questions according to your interest and time.

1 Arguments over religion make many of us uncomfortable. Why? Does Paul's letter so far make for uncomfortable reading?

2 What watered-down or distorted versions of the gospel are promoted today? How can one distinguish between authentic and inauthentic explanations of who Jesus is, what he has done, and what he means for our lives?

3 In discussions of religious differences, when is it best to look for the common ground? When is it best to point out the differences?

4 Do people who have a dramatic spiritual experience like Paul's have a deeper knowledge of God than people who do not have such an experience? Explain your reasoning.

5 What is the gospel? That is the central question in Paul's letter to the Galatians. What is your understanding of the gospel? Which elements of the gospel are expressed in the opening of Paul's letter (1:1–5)? What other aspects of the gospel would you add to his statement?

6 How has your life been affected by your belief that God raised Jesus from the dead (1:1)? What implications does Jesus' resurrection have for you in the present season of your life?

7 Paul realized that he had been going in the wrong direction (1:13–17). When have you had this kind of experience? What did you learn about yourself? How does that lesson affect you today?

Like a person, the Bible has depths unplumbed, secrets untold, layers beyond layers, a will and a presence that, taken together, defy any pretense of having it in one's pocket, even if someone . . . were to commit the whole thing to memory.

H. A. Nielsen, *The Bible—As If for the First Time*

Approach to Prayer

15 minutes
Use this approach—or create your own!

◆ Let one member of the group
read aloud John 17:6–26, Jesus'
prayer for his followers to be
kept in the truth and love of God.
Pause for silent reflection. Then
pray Psalm 145, a celebration
of God's faithfulness in guarding
and protecting his people.

Living Tradition

Guided by the Spirit

This section is a supplement for individual reading.

The Galatian Christians were in a difficult spot. Paul had told them one thing about Christ. Now other Christian teachers were telling them something different. Paul had taught them that gentile Christians do not need to follow the Mosaic Law, but the other teachers were warning them that if they did not follow the Mosaic Law they would forfeit their relationship with God. This warning had the Galatians in anguish (in 1:7 Paul speaks of the other teachers "confusing," or frightening the Galatians).

How could the Galatians find the right path? The other teachers claimed to represent the views of the apostles in Jerusalem. Paul insisted that *he* was authorized directly by Jesus. The Galatians were new Christians, yet already they had to sort through complex issues in a profound theological controversy.

And they did. We have no details about how the conflict was resolved, but we know the outcome. The Christians in Galatia and throughout the early Church eventually recognized the truth of Paul's message. Paul's letter to the Galatians, rather than any writings of those who opposed him, was acknowledged as a reflection of the faith of the Church—as can be seen from the fact that it was incorporated in the New Testament. Behind this development, steering the sometimes confused communities of Christians through theologically troubled waters, was the Holy Spirit. By the presence of the Spirit, Jesus did not allow his followers to go astray from him (see John 16:12–15).

This experience has been repeated many times in the history of the Church. Controversies have arisen, sometimes causing great confusion and anguish. But the Spirit has guided the Church to an understanding of the truth, although the process has not always been tidy. The bishops at Vatican Council II (1962–65) expressed confidence that the Spirit will always guide the Church. Despite the mistakes, misunderstandings, and sins of individual members, even of those in the highest positions of leadership, Jesus will continue to protect his body, the Church. The bishops called this "the Church's charism of infallibility"—its protection by the Spirit from error in all that it teaches in the name of Christ (*Dogmatic Constitution on the Church,* section 25).

Between Discussions

Two Ages of History

Greeting the Galatians, Paul speaks of "the Lord Jesus Christ, who gave himself for our sins to set us free from the present evil age" (1:3–4). It is easy to sail past this little statement. Yet it gives us valuable background for understanding Paul's entire letter.

The first part of Paul's statement, about Jesus giving himself "for our sins," focuses on Jesus' laying down his life to bring each of us God's forgiveness. In the second part, by speaking of Jesus setting us free from "the present evil age," Paul broadens the focus beyond individuals. He takes in the whole of history, summing it up as an "evil age." Thus Paul puts Jesus' saving love for individuals within the big picture of the condition of human society as a whole.

When a person speaks about a "present evil age," you might suppose that he or she believes there is also another, better age to come. That is, indeed, the structure of Paul's thought. He never actually uses the term "the age to come." But he refers to it by another term: the "new creation" (6:15).

Already before the time of Jesus, many Jews viewed God's dealings with the human race as falling into two distinct periods— the present age, filled with problems, and a future age, when God would set everything right. This view emerges in the book of Daniel (Daniel 7:9–14, 27). Jesus embraced it explicitly, speaking of "this age" and "the age to come" (Matthew 12:32; Mark 10:30; compare Luke 20:34–35).

First-century Jews who shared this belief in two ages generally expected God to bring the present age to a close through a decisive confrontation with evil, after which he would bring in a final, glorious period of human existence. Jesus adjusted this view. By his death and resurrection, he did meet and defeat the powers of evil and began the restoration of creation—but without bringing the "present" age to an end. Jesus brought the final age *into* the present age. The final age—what Paul calls the "new creation"— has begun; those who believe in Jesus already enter into it and begin to experience Jesus' victory over the powers of evil. Yet the present age continues, and the ultimate effects of Jesus' victory are not yet fully manifested.

By saying that the present age is evil, Paul does not mean that creation is bad. As St. Thomas Aquinas explained, Paul calls this age evil "on account of the evils which are in it." A modern commentator, James D. G. Dunn, explains, "Paul certainly had no doubts that the present age was marked by corruptibility, superficiality, folly, and blindness . . . or that humankind as heirs of Adam were caught under the reign of sin and death." In Paul's view, sin and death are not mere occurrences; they are mighty powers actively working against human beings. In Paul's view, the problem of evil that we face is not simply a matter of our own individual moral failings. Various evil powers are at work in the world. Paul speaks mysteriously of elemental forces that hold human beings under their sway (4:3–9) and of "the flesh," which he views as a more-than-merely-human evil power seeking to dominate human beings.

Paul's thinking, which reflects his first-century Greek and Hebrew culture, is somewhat foreign to us. But we are familiar with the idea that the evil in human history is something more than the sum of the individuals' bad decisions. When we consider the enduring power of evil institutions such as slavery, the vast destructions wrought by totalitarian ideologies, the frightful slaughters spurred by ethnic hatreds, or terrorism, it is easy to share Paul's conviction that dark forces are at work beneath the surface of human events. Our own individual struggles with stubborn sins may also lead us to suspect that we are entangled in evils that are bigger than ourselves.

Paul is convinced that the powers of evil at work in human society in "the present evil age" cannot be defeated by human resources alone. To attain the holiness God intends for us, we need more than God's forgiveness and more than a program of discipline. Not even the Mosaic Law, Paul will argue, has the power to overcome the forces of evil in the world. Only Christ, by his death and resurrection, and the power of his Spirit can set us free.

CRUCIAL EVENTS

Questions to Begin

15 minutes
Use a question or two to get warmed up for the reading.

1 When have you been involved in something where success depended on teamwork?

2 When have you been criticized for changing your mind?

3 When have you been nervous going into a meeting?

If anything could sustain and support a wise person in this life or help him or her to preserve peace of mind amid the conflicts of the world, it is, I reckon, meditation on and knowledge of the Bible.

St. Jerome, *On Ephesians*

5 minutes
Read the passage aloud. Let individuals take turns reading paragraphs.

The Reading: Galatians 1:11–2:16

Paul's Early Ministry (A Review of Last Week's Account)

11 For I want you to know, brothers and sisters, that the gospel that was proclaimed by me is not of human origin; 12 for I did not receive it from a human source, nor was I taught it, but I received it through a revelation of Jesus Christ. . . .

15 But when God, who had set me apart before I was born and called me through his grace, was pleased 16 to reveal his Son to me, so that I might proclaim him among the Gentiles, I did not confer with any human being, 17 nor did I go up to Jerusalem to those who were already apostles before me, but I went away at once into Arabia, and afterwards I returned to Damascus.

18 Then after three years I did go up to Jerusalem to visit Cephas and stayed with him fifteen days; 19 but I did not see any other apostle except James the Lord's brother. 20 In what I am writing to you, before God, I do not lie! 21 Then I went into the regions of Syria and Cilicia, 22 and I was still unknown by sight to the churches of Judea that are in Christ. . . .

Consultation in Jerusalem

2:1 Then after fourteen years I went up again to Jerusalem with Barnabas, taking Titus along with me. 2 I went up in response to a revelation. Then I laid before them (though only in a private meeting with the acknowledged leaders) the gospel that I proclaim among the Gentiles, in order to make sure that I was not running, or had not run, in vain.

3 But even Titus, who was with me, was not compelled to be circumcised, though he was a Greek. 4 But because of false believers secretly brought in, who slipped in to spy on the freedom we have in Christ Jesus, so that they might enslave us— 5 we did not submit to them even for a moment, so that the truth of the gospel might always remain with you. 6 And from those who were supposed to be acknowledged leaders (what they actually were makes no difference to me; God shows no partiality)—those leaders contributed nothing to me.

7 On the contrary, when they saw that I had been entrusted with the gospel for the uncircumcised, just as Peter had been entrusted with the gospel for the circumcised 8 (for he who worked through Peter making him an apostle to the circumcised also worked through me in sending me to the Gentiles), 9 and when James and Cephas and John, who were acknowledged pillars, recognized the grace that had been given to me, they gave to Barnabas and me the right hand of fellowship, agreeing that we should go to the Gentiles and they to the circumcised.

10 They asked only one thing, that we remember the poor, which was actually what I was eager to do.

Confrontation in Antioch

11 But when Cephas came to Antioch, I opposed him to his face, because he stood self-condemned; 12 for until certain people came from James, he used to eat with the Gentiles. But after they came, he drew back and kept himself separate for fear of the circumcision faction. 13 And the other Jews joined him in this hypocrisy, so that even Barnabas was led astray by their hypocrisy. 14 But when I saw that they were not acting consistently with the truth of the gospel, I said to Cephas before them all, "If you, though a Jew, live like a Gentile and not like a Jew, how can you compel the Gentiles to live like Jews?"

15 We ourselves are Jews by birth and not Gentile sinners; 16 yet we know that a person is justified not by the works of the law but through faith in Jesus Christ. And we have come to believe in Christ Jesus, so that we might be justified by faith in Christ, and not by doing the works of the law, because no one will be justified by the works of the law.

10 minutes
Choose questions according to your interest and time.

1 Paul describes how he related at first to Peter and to the other leaders of the Church in Jerusalem (1:11–22). How would you describe this relationship in a word or two?

2 How did the relationship change in 2:1–10?

3 How did the relationship change in 2:11–16?

4 What was it that none of the leaders in Jerusalem "contributed" to Paul (2:6)?

5 How do you think Peter might have responded to Paul's rebuke in 2:13–16?

6 What impression of Paul do you get from our readings so far? (Point to specific verses to support your view.)

A Guide to the Reading

*If participants have not read this section already, read it aloud.
Otherwise go on to "Questions for Application."*

2:1–10. In the face of allegations that his version of the gospel is not authorized or authentic, Paul's first concern is to show that he came to know Jesus directly and received the gospel directly from Jesus. This is the point of Paul's recounting of events. He received his understanding of Jesus not through other people, not even through the apostles in Jerusalem, but from Jesus himself (1:11–16). The other apostles neither instructed him nor commissioned him (1:16–22). Furthermore, they eventually recognized that his gospel came from God (2:1–10).

For years, Paul preached Jesus to non-Jews without requiring them to become Jews and keep the Mosaic Law (2:1–10). Undoubtedly he was aware that this policy put him at odds with many Jewish Christians. But since he was sure that his policy was authorized by the Lord, he did not feel the need for others' approval, not even the approval of Jesus' original disciples (1:15–22). Yet, in a sense, Paul *did* need their approval, not in order to know whether his preaching was true, but in order for it to succeed (2:2). If the leaders of the mother church in Jerusalem did not acknowledge that Paul's Law-free gospel came from God, a chasm would open up between the predominantly Jewish communities of believers and the gentile Christian communities. God's intention of uniting Jews and non-Jews in Christ would be frustrated. Paul's mission would be a failure.

To avoid this danger, Paul goes to Jerusalem to obtain the approval of the leaders of the mother church (2:1–2). But while he wishes to secure their approval, he does not wish to admit that, in principle, he needs it. Thus his visit—and his account of it—is a balancing act. He acknowledges the authority of the leaders in Jerusalem: they are the "pillars" of the Church (2:9); yet he speaks as though he is their equal before God (2:6). He is glad to report that the Jerusalem leaders did not call for any change in his policy toward gentiles (2:3, 6). Yet he does not want the Galatians to think that his policy needs any validation (2:5); it is, after all, "the truth of the gospel." He wants the Galatians to know that the Jerusalem leaders accepted his mission to gentiles (2:7–9). Yet he does not grant that they *authorized* him; they simply *recognized* that God had already appointed him to his ministry.

Going up to Jerusalem, Paul takes along a Jewish-Christian colleague named Barnabas (perhaps he mentions him because the Galatians know him personally) and an assistant named Titus, who is a gentile Christian and uncircumcised. Bringing Titus is a bold step. Titus represents all the gentiles who have become Christians through Paul's preaching and have not embraced the Mosaic Law. Paul is confident that, in Christ, God now fully accepts these gentiles as sons and daughters. By bringing Titus into the Jewish-Christian mother church in Jerusalem, Paul challenges the leaders there to recognize God's action through Christ among the gentiles. Paul is playing for high stakes. Will the leaders in Jerusalem accept Titus *as he is?* If they insist that Titus be circumcised, Paul and Titus will refuse—and the Jewish and gentile missions will be split apart from each other.

Some conflict occurred in connection with the meeting in Jerusalem (2:4–5), although whether in Jerusalem or beforehand in Antioch is not clear. Whoever the "false believers" were, Peter, James, and John were not among them. These false believers spied on the others' freedom—probably they observed the freedom of the gentile believers not to follow the Mosaic Law and the freedom of the Jewish believers to associate closely with the gentile believers. Just recalling the machinations of these false brethren raises Paul's blood pressure and makes him sputter with indignation. His sentences begin to break down. The dashes in 2:4–6 are the translators' way of trying to connect Paul's fragmented thoughts.

Much to Paul's relief, the leaders in Jerusalem do not pressure him to add anything to his preaching of the good news about Jesus. In other words, they do not require Titus, or other gentile believers, present and future, to be circumcised and follow the rest of the Mosaic Law.

What led the Jerusalem leaders to take this momentous step was the evidence of God's action in Paul's ministry and the lives of the gentile believers (2:7–9). Indeed, it is amazing how much importance these early Christians gave in their decision making to the visible activity of the Spirit (compare 3:2–5).

2:11–16. Paul's account shifts suddenly from Jerusalem to Antioch. He does not say exactly what was happening in the church in Antioch before the messengers from James arrived, but we may surmise. Peter and other Jewish believers were keeping a kosher kitchen at home but were accepting invitations to dine with gentile brethren who served food that did not meet the requirements of the Mosaic Law.

The representatives from James (2:12) were not "false believers" who opposed the agreement in Jerusalem, for James had assented to that agreement. They were not coming to force the gentiles to be circumcised but simply to urge Peter to stop dining with the gentile believers. Probably they pointed out to Peter that his fraternizing with gentiles was seen as scandalous back in Jerusalem. It was hampering the evangelization of Jews by exposing the Jewish Christians to the charge that they led Jews to abandon the Mosaic Law. An additional factor may have been the existence of Jewish militants in Palestine, who regarded Jews who adopted gentile ways as traitors. The believers in Jerusalem may have been afraid that Peter's liberal dining policy would provoke persecution by these Jewish freedom fighters (see 6:12).

Peter accepted James's advice and withdrew from table fellowship with the gentile believers. The other Jewish Christians followed suit. Since the Eucharist was celebrated in the course of a shared meal, it is possible that the Jewish believers withdrew even from sharing the Eucharist with the gentile believers.

In the minds of Peter and those who followed him, their walkout must have seemed like a reasonable compromise. Yet it treated the gentile believers like second-class citizens in the Church. Inevitably, the gentiles would experience the walkout as pressure to embrace the Mosaic Law.

Perhaps Peter did not grasp the effects that his withdrawal would have on the gentile Christians. But Paul did. The problem was a public one in the community, so he publicly confronted Peter about his behavior. Paul recognized the importance of adapting to local circumstances (1 Corinthians 9:19–23). But he insisted that *no* adaptation must be allowed to compromise the good news that God offers every man and woman a full relationship with himself through Jesus his Son. Paul states this principle at the end of his account (2:15–16). In the next section of his letter, he will move from reporting on past events to explaining the issues involved in the controversy over the gospel.

Regarding the conclusion of this week's reading (2:16), New Testament scholar James D. G. Dunn makes this remark: "It has to be noted that he does *not* say that Peter accepted his rebuke and resumed his former practice. Paul would almost certainly have noted this further victory for his understanding of the gospel, had he been able to win Peter over, just as he obviously took pains to describe his earlier victory in Jerusalem."

At least for a time, Paul's Law-free approach to the gospel may not have won out at Antioch. As he writes to the Galatians, Paul may be concerned that it will not win out in Galatia either. From our much later point of view, we know that the whole Church eventually recognized Paul's understanding of the gospel as correct. But Paul could not foresee that outcome. His letter shows him torn between discouragement and hope (1:6; 3:1; 4:11, 20; 5:9–10). Undoubtedly it is a struggle that all of us can appreciate.

And what about Peter? Throughout the Gospels and Acts of the Apostles, Peter is portrayed as a man who loves Jesus deeply and is determined to follow him, but who is rather often slow to perceive what Jesus is about (Mark 1:35–38; 8:31–33; 9:5–6). Yet Peter is a learner, a man willing to change as the Lord makes his will plain. The New Testament writings say nothing more about Peter's approach to the question of gentiles' place in the Church and their relationship to the Mosaic Law. But it may well be that Peter and Paul reached agreement on the subject. In a later letter, Paul mentions Peter without any hint that he and Peter do not see eye to eye on Christian teaching (1 Corinthians 1:12; 3:22; 9:5). An early tradition holds that the two men died at about the same time, as martyrs in Rome. Did these two great leaders of the early Church meet one last time in Rome before giving their lives in witness to their Lord?

Questions for Application

40 minutes
Choose questions according to your interest and time.

1   What undermines unity in your parish? What could be done to draw different groups of people closer together?

2   Paul is sensitive to the feelings of the gentile Christians at Antioch who may have felt that the Jewish Christians were treating them as unacceptable. Who might feel like second-class citizens in your parish? Does anyone speak up for them? What could be done to remedy the problem?

3   Paul is worried about the Galatians. What have you learned about living with anxiety over the well-being of those who are close to you? Does Paul's example offer insights into how to handle such anxiety?

4   In order to know God's will, the leaders of the early Church sought to discern what the Holy Spirit was doing. How can a person apply this principle in their personal search to know God's will? How can a parish or other Christian group apply this principle? How can people detect God's action in their lives and circumstances?

5 Everyone at times faces accusations and criticisms. What can be learned from Paul about how to respond?

6 Paul confronted Peter before the community in Antioch (2:14). When is it best to handle a disagreement privately? When is it best to bring it out in the open? What experiences have helped you learn about this?

7 Paul speaks of being set apart by God for his service from the womb (1:15). When have you had the sense of discovering the purposes for which God created you? What could you do to seek a clearer understanding of his will for you?

8 For personal reflection: Paul recounts significant events in his relationship with Christ and in the work Christ gave him to do. If you were to assemble a list of significant events in your own relationship with God, what would you put on the list? What pattern emerges from these events? What can you learn about God's relationship with you? about how he wishes you to respond to him?

Approach to Prayer

15 minutes
Use this approach—or create your own!

◆ Pray two psalms for the peace
and unity of the Church: Psalms
122 and 133. End with a Glory
to the Father.

Saints in the Making

Dear Pope . . .

This section is a supplement for individual reading.

In Antioch, St. Paul spoke sharply to St. Peter. "Stop being a hypocrite," he said. "Overcome your fears and do what you know you ought to do" (see 2:11–14).

The successors of Peter have not been immune to fear. Popes are human; sometimes they have needed confrontational help to do the right thing. Pope Gregory XI was one of these.

In 1305, Pope Clement V had moved temporarily from Rome to Avignon, in southern France, to deal with ecclesiastical and political problems. But Clement never went back; and his successors stayed on in Avignon. The Avignon popes pursued contradictory policies, reforming abuses in the Church while building their palace in Avignon into the most splendid and luxurious court in Europe. In their absence, central Italy, where the papacy possessed considerable territory, fell into chaos. When Gregory became pope in 1370, he resolved, for the good of the Church, and of the Italians, to return to Rome.

But he hesitated. Powerful figures in France sought to hold him back. Fear for his personal safety in Italy made him waver. Six years after his election, he was still delaying in Avignon.

At this point, a young woman named Catherine, from Siena, Italy, took it on herself to play Paul in Gregory's life. She wrote to him, telling him in no uncertain terms to carry through on his decision. "Come, come; don't resist any longer the will of God who is calling you!" Catherine demanded in a letter in February 1376. "The starving little sheep are waiting for you to come and take possession of the place of your predecessor and model, the apostle Peter. You, as Christ's vicar, ought to be residing in your proper place. Come! Come! Come! Don't put it off any longer! Take heart, and don't be afraid of anything that might happen, for God will be with you."

A month later she wrote: "Be a courageous man for me, not a coward. Respond to God, who is calling you to come and take possession of the place of the glorious shepherd!"

Catherine kept up her drumbeat of reproaches and reassurances month after month. Finally, in September, she tipped the balance. Gregory left Avignon. By early 1377, the bishop of Rome was home again among his flock.

After her death in 1380, Catherine was declared a saint.

Between Discussions

Two Terms That Cause Distress

A t the end of our last reading, Paul declared, "A person is justified not by the works of the law but through faith in Jesus Christ" (2:16). Two of the terms Paul uses in this statement have caused interpreters no end of trouble. What does Paul mean by "justified"? And what are "the works of the law"? Both terms play an important part in the case Paul is about to present, so it will be useful to pause and consider what he does and does not mean by them.

The Greek word translated "justify" was often used in courtrooms. A judge who determined that a defendant did not commit the crime of which he or she was accused would "justify" the defendant, that is, he would declare the defendant not guilty. To be justified was to be acquitted, to have one's innocence vindicated.

When Paul says that God justifies us through our faith in Jesus, he means that God acquits us of the sins of which we are accused, he declares us to be innocent. But Paul gives the term a new twist. The twist is that it is not false accusations that God overthrows, but true ones. We *are* sinners. God does not declare innocent those who are innocent but those who are guilty. God knows well how guilty the defendants are, but in Christ he acquits us nonetheless.

The question is whether this is simply a policy of *acceptance* on God's part, or something more. Does God decide to treat us in Christ *as though* we were innocent, to relate to us as though we were something we are not? Or, by justifying us, does God also change us? Beginning with Martin Luther in the sixteenth century, many Christians have understood Paul to mean that being justified simply gives us a new standing before God. By justifying us, it is thought, God brings us into relationship with himself and begins to treat us the way he treats his Son—as his sons and daughters— even though we are still the same thoroughgoing sinners we always were. But there are reasons to think that, in Paul's view, God does much more than this when he justifies us in Christ.

First, there is Paul's use of the Greek word translated "justification," the noun that corresponds to the Greek verb *justify* (2:21). The Greek word translated "justification" corresponds to a

Hebrew word in the Old Testament that is often translated "righteousness." In the Old Testament, *righteousness* means *being* righteous, being upright in one's character and relationships. Righteousness does involve being acceptable to God, but never apart from being an upright person. If being justified gives a person righteousness, it means more than giving him or her a new status before God; it also means setting the person right, making the person right. When God justifies us, he changes us. He not only *declares* us to be just; he *makes* us so (see 2 Corinthians 5:21). New Testament scholar E. P. Sanders suggests that we can bring out Paul's meaning by stretching the English language and saying that, in Christ, God not only declares us to have the status of a righteous person, he "righteouses" us.

Second, by using a range of other terms to express what God does for us through Christ, Paul shows that his understanding of being justified by God is not external, a matter of status, but internal, a matter of a personal change. Paul connects being justified with

- having Christ living in oneself as one's personal center (2:20)
- being snatched out of the power of evil forces (3:13; 4:3–5)
- receiving the Holy Spirit as God's adopted sons and daughters (4:4–7)

These parallel statements show that, for Paul, being justified by God means being freed from evil power and being made alive by God through the inner presence of Christ and his Holy Spirit. This presence of the Son and the Spirit draws us into the "new creation" that has begun through Jesus' death and resurrection (see 6:15).

Of course, being justified by God in Christ does not totally transform us. We continue to sin. Being justified is both the beginning of a personal revolution and a goal toward which we are moving with the help of the Spirit. Paul speaks of justification as something both already received (2:16) and yet to be hoped for (5:5). Thus, at present, it is a process of being set right by God. We have entered into a new relationship with God; we have been and are being changed; we look forward to being changed completely. God is making us into men and women who will truly and fully be deserving of the verdict *righteous* at the final judgment, who have become the kind of persons who will be at home with God for all eternity because he will have made us like himself (see 1 John 3:2).

What about the term "the works of the law"? This is sometimes interpreted to mean, in a general way, "what God commands." Thus Paul's statement that we are not justified by the works of the law is taken to mean that our own human efforts to do what God commands cannot save us; only God's grace saves us. When Paul's words are interpreted this way, he seems to be emphasizing the difference between human deeds and faith in God's actions. But this misses Paul's point.

For the most part in Galatians, "the law" refers specifically to the Law of Moses. To grasp Paul's point when he says we are not saved by "the works of the law," it is important to remember that the Law of Moses involves an entire way of life—not only moral principles (Exodus 20:1–17) but also liturgical instructions (Exodus 25–31), precepts governing symbolic religious behavior (Leviticus 11–15; 19:26), cultural practices (Numbers 27:1–11), and so on. In Galatians, doing "the works of the law" refers especially to following some prominent rules in the Mosaic Law that distinguished Jews from gentiles and reinforced Jews' sense of living in a covenant with God: circumcision, dietary practices, Sabbath, festivals, and rules about the clean and unclean status of persons and objects. The question is whether gentile Christians have to embrace these particular practices, as well as the rest of the Mosaic package.

In the light of Christ, Paul came to see the inadequacy of the Mosaic Law as a framework for a relationship with God. He experienced firsthand that Jesus can accomplish in a person more than the Mosaic Law. The Spirit given by Jesus is infinitely more capable of accomplishing the process of setting us right than "the works of the law," that is, the pattern of life in the Law of Moses.

Thus Paul is not setting up a contrast between obedience to God and faith in God. His contrast is between relating to God within the framework of the Law of Moses and relating to God within the framework of a personal relationship with Jesus. Paul is not contrasting (a) a relationship of faith, trust, and confidence in God with (b) human actions, good deeds, works of mercy, or efforts to carry out God's will. This becomes clear further on in the letter when Paul speaks about "faith *working* through love" and about "*obeying* the truth" (5:6–7, emphasis added). Paul is not setting up a contrast between believing and obeying, but between following the Mosaic Law and having faith in Jesus.

Since the Protestant Reformation, many Christians have interpreted Paul's reference to "works" to mean people's own efforts to achieve salvation, set in sharp contrast to the grace of God in Christ working in people entirely through faith. This interpretation has led Protestants to reject aspects of Catholic life (the Mass, practices such as fasting, monastic life), which seem to them to be based on a mistaken conviction that Christians can earn their way to heaven. Catholics do not in fact believe that people can earn their way to heaven. The Catholic Church has never taught that people can earn their salvation. Following Paul, the Church teaches that we are saved by God's grace, but that our own—grace-enabled—response to God is a crucial part of the process (see the *Catechism of the Catholic Church,* sections 1996–2001, 2008–09).

Unfortunately, the English terms often used to translate Paul's statement in 2:16 tend to obscure his meaning. In ordinary speech, to *justify* means "to offer a rationale" (Ellen justified her absence from work by explaining that she had to pick up her daughter from school). *Righteous* tends to sound like *self-righteous.* The term *works* seems to emphasize a contrast between human deeds and God's grace. The word *law* may seem to refer generally to God's will for human behavior. To avoid these mis-impressions, in this guide I will generally speak of God "setting us right" and will avoid the words *justify, justification, righteous,* and *works.* I have been capitalizing *Law* as a reminder that in general Paul is speaking about the Law of Moses.

FAITH AND BLESSING

Questions to Begin

15 minutes
Use a question or two to get warmed up for the reading.

1 Among your ancestors and the older members of your family, who do you take as a model?

2 When you were very little, where did you think God lived?

5 minutes
Read the passage aloud. Let individuals take turns reading
paragraphs.

The Reading: Galatians 2:15–3:14

The Heart of Paul's Message

15 We ourselves are Jews by birth and not Gentile sinners; 16 yet
we know that a person is justified not by the works of the law but
through faith in Jesus Christ. And we have come to believe in Christ
Jesus, so that we might be justified by faith in Christ, and not by
doing the works of the law, because no one will be justified by the
works of the law.

17 But if, in our effort to be justified in Christ, we ourselves
have been found to be sinners, is Christ then a servant of sin?
Certainly not! 18 But if I build up again the very things that I once
tore down, then I demonstrate that I am a transgressor. 19 For
through the law I died to the law, so that I might live to God. I have
been crucified with Christ; 20 and it is no longer I who live, but it is
Christ who lives in me. And the life I now live in the flesh I live by
faith in the Son of God, who loved me and gave himself for me.
21 I do not nullify the grace of God; for if justification comes
through the law, then Christ died for nothing.

An Appeal to Experience

1 You foolish Galatians! Who has bewitched you? It was before your
eyes that Jesus Christ was publicly exhibited as crucified! 2 The only
thing I want to learn from you is this: Did you receive the Spirit by
doing the works of the law or by believing what you heard? 3 Are you
so foolish? Having started with the Spirit, are you now ending with
the flesh? 4 Did you experience so much for nothing?—if it really was
for nothing. 5 Well then, does God supply you with the Spirit and
work miracles among you by your doing the works of the law, or by
your believing what you heard?

How to Receive God's Blessing

6 Just as Abraham "believed God, and it was reckoned to him as
righteousness," 7 so, you see, those who believe are the descendants of
Abraham. 8 And the scripture, foreseeing that God would justify the
Gentiles by faith, declared the gospel beforehand to Abraham, saying,

"All the Gentiles shall be blessed in you." [9] For this reason, those who believe are blessed with Abraham who believed.

The Blessing Comes through Christ

[10] For all who rely on the works of the law are under a curse; for it is written, "Cursed is everyone who does not observe and obey all the things written in the book of the law." [11] Now it is evident that no one is justified before God by the law; for "The one who is righteous will live by faith." [12] But the law does not rest on faith; on the contrary, "Whoever does the works of the law will live by them." [13] Christ redeemed us from the curse of the law by becoming a curse for us—for it is written, "Cursed is everyone who hangs on a tree"— [14] in order that in Christ Jesus the blessing of Abraham might come to the Gentiles, so that we might receive the promise of the Spirit through faith.

10 minutes
Choose questions according to your interest and time.

1 How would you express in your own words the meaning of Paul's statement in 2:20?

2 Paul does not say simply that the Galatians are *mistaken* but that they are "foolish" (3:1). Why? What does Paul see as the antidote to their foolishness?

3 What did the Galatians experience from the Holy Spirit (3:4; compare 5:22–23)?

4 If the Galatians answer Paul's question (3:5) as he expects they will, what conclusion will they draw regarding whether they need to begin following the whole Mosaic Law?

5 What similarity can you detect between the Jerusalem leaders' reasoning in 2:7–9 and Paul's reasoning in 3:2–5?

6 By putting together 3:2–5, 9, and 14, what would you conclude is a key element of the "blessing" that Paul discusses in this section?

A Guide to the Reading

*If participants have not read this section already, read it aloud.
Otherwise go on to "Questions for Application."*

It is not clear where Paul leaves off his account of his confrontation with Peter in Antioch, but by the beginning of chapter 3 we sense that Paul is no longer quoting his words to Peter on that occasion. He is now presenting his understanding of the gospel directly to the Galatians.

2:15–16. For a moment Paul abandons his confrontational tone and looks for common ground between himself and Peter (and the Jewish Christian teachers who are disturbing the Galatians). "Look," he says in a friendly way, "we Jews know some things about God that gentiles do not. Without the Mosaic Law to guide them, gentiles fall into some sins from which the Law protects us." But suddenly Paul wheels around and makes a fundamental criticism of the Mosaic Law: "God does not make us right through the Mosaic Law, but through Christ!"

At this point, Paul begins a lengthy negative comparison of the Mosaic Law and Christ. These are two ways in which God has revealed himself to human beings, each with its characteristic human response. Keeping the Mosaic Law is, by definition, a law-centered response to God. As such it places an emphasis on carefully observing precepts and regulations (Paul used to be a model of this way of relating to God: see 1:14). Faith in Jesus is a person-centered response to God. It is characterized by being attentive to Jesus, imitating him, relinquishing one's will to him, taking him as the center of one's existence, allowing oneself to be guided by his Spirit.

Both modes of response to God involve faith. Many passages in Scripture show that keeping the Mosaic Law can be a heartfelt, trusting response to God (Psalm 119). It is also plain in Scripture that God's grace is at work in those who follow the Mosaic Law. But Paul here ignores the faith dimension of keeping the Mosaic Law in order to emphasize that God's action through Jesus is infinitely greater—and in order to persuade the gentile Galatians not to embrace the Mosaic Law.

2:17–18. Paul has encouraged Jewish Christians to eat at the tables of gentile Christians whose food is unacceptable according to the dietary rules in the Mosaic Law. In the eyes of some Jews, such dining is sinful. Is Christ, then, leading Jews into sin (2:17)? On the contrary, Paul replies, it would be leading them into sin to encourage them to go back to keeping the dietary laws in a way that excludes their gentile brothers and sisters in Christ— exactly what Paul accuses Peter of doing. The real sin, in Paul's view, is to insist that the Mosaic Law is necessary for a relationship with God, because this implies that Christ is not enough.

2:19–20. "I have been crucified with Christ," Paul declares, "and it is no longer I who live, but it is Christ who lives in me. And the life I now live in the flesh I live by faith in the Son of God, who loved me and gave himself for me" (2:19–20). No more profound description of Christian life has ever been made.

"I am no longer I," Paul says paradoxically. "Jesus has shared his death with me and has recreated me as a new person in union with himself." By the form of the Greek verbs, Paul implies that he *has been* and *is still crucified* with Christ, continuing to share in his death, while now continuously sharing in his life. Paul's independent existence has come and continues to come to an end. "Now, in my weakness, I live in Christ, and Christ lives in me, sharing with me his faith in God, his death-conquering death, his risen life."

Paul has died not only to his old self but also to the Mosaic Law. A person's relationship with God cannot have two centers. Either the Mosaic Law or Christ is the center of a person's life. Embracing Christ, Paul has let go of the Mosaic Law.

2:21. Jesus would not have laid down his life if there were already a fully satisfactory way for human beings to share in God's life. The Mosaic Law was good but inadequate. Christ supplies all that was lacking. To suggest that a person who lives in Christ also needs to follow the Law shows a failure to grasp this reality.

3:1–5. Christ brings his Spirit to those who believe in him. The Spirit acts in a wide variety of ways: lifting people out of the ruts of habitual sin, healing bodies and minds, replacing despair with joy. The Galatians already experience these workings of the Spirit (3:4). What more could they possibly gain from following the Mosaic Law?

For the first time in this letter, Paul speaks of "the flesh," a term he uses with more than one meaning. Here "the flesh" refers to the purely human level of existence. Living in the flesh means getting by on human resources without the power of the Spirit. For the Galatians to think that they need the Mosaic Law to complete their relationship with God amounts to a denial of Christ and the Spirit. The Galatians think they will rise up to a higher level and become perfect by following the Mosaic Law. But by thinking that the Mosaic Law is higher than Christ they are actually falling down to a lower level, a level without the Spirit, the level of "the flesh," where perfection will be impossible.

3:6–9, 14. Apparently the other teachers have told the Galatians that God's blessing comes to people through Abraham (Genesis 12:2–3; 17:4; 18:18). "If you wish to experience this blessing," the teachers say, "become his descendants by following his example. Abraham circumcised himself as a sign of his acceptance of God's promise to him. You also must be circumcised in order to receive the promised blessing." Being circumcised is, of course, the sign of a man's becoming a Jew and undertaking to keep the whole Mosaic Law.

In response, Paul reexamines Abraham's relationship with God. God promised Abraham numerous offspring, even though Abraham and his wife, Sarah, were already old. Abraham responded to God with trust and hope; he believed that God is the Creator who brings "into existence the things that do not exist" (Romans 4:17). Against all evidence, he held on to God's promise. This trust brought Abraham into a life-giving relationship with God, who "reckoned it to him as righteousness" (Genesis 15:6).

Since Abraham was a man of faith, Paul argues, it is by faith that gentiles become Abraham's adopted sons and daughters. When they put their faith in Christ, believing that he conquers death and brings a new creation, they become not only sons and daughters of Abraham but sons and daughters of God. They then lack nothing in their relationship with God. Thus, they have no need to follow Abraham's example of circumcision. "Relax," Paul tells the Galatians. "You have received blessing with Abraham the believer by becoming believers yourselves."

3:10, 13. Paul's point is that those who *keep* the Law are under a curse. Why, then, does he quote a passage that says those who do *not* keep the Law are cursed (3:10—Deuteronomy 27:26)? Some commentators suggest that Paul is assuming here that in fact no one *can* keep the whole Law; thus everyone who tries to keep the Law inevitably falls under the curse on those who fail to keep it. Others suggest that Paul thinks that the very attempt to keep the Law is, paradoxically, a violation of the Law, since God wishes to be approached in faith rather than through merely human efforts. Yet the Galatians could hardly have grasped such hidden assumptions unless Paul made them explicit, which he does not.

A better explanation, perhaps, is that Paul seeks to show that those who undertake to follow the Law make themselves liable to being cursed. Paul quotes Deuteronomy 27:26 to demonstrate the Law's cursing power. By dying on a cross (symbolically a "tree") Jesus fell under a curse in the Law (3:13; Deuteronomy 21:23; compare Acts 5:30), further demonstrating the Law's cursing power. The fact that even Jesus, who did not sin, fell under the curse powerfully demonstrates that the Law brings a curse on those who are subject to it. Paul reasons that if the Mosaic Law carries a curse, it cannot be life-giving. Paul grants that a person who follows the Mosaic precepts may in some sense "live by them" (3:12), but that person does not thereby receive the gift of God's life that men and women really need. That gift of life—the Holy Spirit—comes through Christ and is received by faith.

3:11–12. Keeping the Law does not make a person right with God and right within themselves; it does not have the power to transform. Paul does not deny the possibility that some people experienced God's transformative power as they followed the Mosaic Law. His point is that the Law does not by itself bring this power, but Jesus does.

Questions for Application

40 minutes
Choose questions according to your interest and time.

---

1 What does it mean to have Christ in us as the source of life?

---

2 What competes with Jesus for the central place in your life? What can you do to keep him at the center?

---

3 What promises has God made to everyone? Are there any that are especially important to you in this period of your life?

---

4 Can devotions and religious practices be a distraction from Jesus? How can a person know whether these are leading him or her closer to the Lord or away from him?

5 If Paul were to make to you the argument that he makes to the Galatians in 3:2–5, what sorts of experiences might he point to in your life?

6 For personal reflection: Do you think of God primarily as one who promises you good and seeks to bless you, or as one who looms over you, threatening to punish you for your sins?

7 For personal reflection: What part of your life have you found most difficult to change? How could you open up this area of your life to the power of the Holy Spirit?

Bible discussion groups reveal the complementarity between two elements—silence and sharing. The Word of God both touches the depths of the heart and gathers together in fellowship.

The Taizé Community, *Listening with the Heart*

Approach to Prayer

15 minutes
Use this approach—or create your own!

◆ Reread 2:20 aloud. Then read
the following excerpts from
the Gospel of John, pausing
briefly for silent reflection
after each one.

John 6:54–57
John 7:37–38
John 14:23
John 15:4–5

End with the Our Father.

Saints in the Making

Christ Living in Me

This section is a supplement for individual reading.

I mean to be a missionary!" announced fifteen-year-old John Gabriel Perboyre after hearing a sermon on foreign missions. The young Frenchman believed God was calling him to take the gospel to China. At the age of twenty-four he was ordained a priest in the Congregation of the Mission. But instead of being sent to China, he was assigned to serve in the order's seminary system. "He knew how to bide his time," one of his students said. "His zeal was unhurried." This applied both to his gentleness in dealing with his students and to his patience in waiting to be sent abroad.

Finally, at the age of thirty-three, his order sent him to China. For several years he cared for abandoned children in Honan and Hupeh. During a persecution of European missionaries, he was arrested and subjected to extreme tortures. After a year of suffering, on September 11, 1840, he was strangled along with several criminals—"a martyrdom fitting for a saint who wanted so much to be like Jesus," one writer observes. He was thirty-eight.

Years before, Perboyre penned a meditation on Galatians 2:20 that expressed his deepest aspirations—a meditation that he prayed often over the years.

O my divine Savior, transform me into yourself. May my hands be the hands of Jesus. May my tongue be the tongue of Jesus. Grant that every faculty of my body may serve only to glorify you. Above all transform my soul and all its powers, so that my memory, will, and affections may be the memory, will, and affections of Jesus. I pray you to destroy in me all that is not of you. Grant that I may live but in you and by you and for you, so that I may truly say with Saint Paul, "It is no longer I, but Christ living in me."

Between Discussions

Two Other Important Terms

Paul is about to use two terms unfamiliar to most of us modern readers. Let's get ready for them.

The first term is simple enough. In 3:24–25 Paul compares the Mosaic Law to a "disciplinarian." The Greek word that Paul uses has given us our English word *pedagogue*. The English word means "teacher," but that is not exactly the meaning of the Greek word.

In ancient Greek society the pedagogue was a familiar figure. The pedagogue was a slave who accompanied a freeborn boy to school and back, carrying the boy's books and protecting him from accidents and incidents along the way.

Outside of school, the pedagogue was the busy parents' solution to the problem of the latchkey child. He supervised the boy's behavior. He taught the boy good manners. He drilled the boy's homework lessons with him. He kept his young charge out of trouble. In general, the pedagogue accompanied the boy wherever he went from the time he left the nursery to the time he entered puberty.

Thus the Greek pedagogue was not so much a teacher as a supervisor—a "disciplinarian," as the New Revised Standard Version puts it.

The second term is a little more difficult to pin down. Paul speaks of the "elemental spirits" of the world (4:3, 9). In Paul's view, before the coming of Christ, people were enslaved by these elemental spirits. If the Galatians submit to the Law of Moses, Paul warns them, they will put themselves once again under the power of these elemental spirits.

The Greek word translated "elemental spirits" could refer to the basic substances of which the world is composed—earth, water, air, and fire, in the thinking of the ancient Greeks. The term could refer to elementary forms of religion. And, among other things, the term could mean the heavenly bodies, that is, the planets and stars, which were thought to control human destiny.

Many ancient thinkers viewed the universe as a place heavily influenced by dark forces. It was a widespread opinion that the basic building blocks of the world—the material substances—

are also demonic forces arrayed against human beings. Similarly, the heavenly bodies were thought to exercise a malignant power over human lives. Hans Dieter Betz, a New Testament scholar, explains that, in the first century, "the common understanding was that man is hopelessly and helplessly engulfed and oppressed by these forces. They play capricious games with man from the time of his entering into the world until his departure. While working inside of man, they make up the body, yet they also encounter him from the outside, in that he has terrible and traumatic experiences of whatever" bad luck has in store.

This way of viewing the universe seems alien to our modern way of thinking, although even today many people suspect that the stars and planets can bring unhappiness to humans, and the idea of bad luck has not quite disappeared from people's minds.

There is no way to know what particular picture of the world Paul has in mind when he uses the term "elemental spirits." But clearly he sees them as cosmic forces hostile to human beings that contribute to the troubles of "the present evil age" (1:4). As we will see, Paul is not at all pessimistic about our situation in relation to the elemental spirits. He does warn the Galatians that they are foolish to put their trust in the Mosaic Law to deliver them from the powers of evil at work in the world. The Law cannot overcome these powers. But Christ can.

FREEDOM THE LAW COULD NOT GIVE

Questions to Begin

15 minutes
Use a question or two to get warmed up for the reading.

1 When you die, what legacy would you like to leave behind? To whom would you like to leave it?

2 What childhood restriction are you particularly glad you no longer have to live under?

5 minutes
Read the passage aloud. Let individuals take turns reading
paragraphs.

The Reading: Galatians 3:15–4:20

Nothing Can Stop God from Fulfilling His Promise

[15] Brothers and sisters, I give an example from daily life: once a
person's will has been ratified, no one adds to it or annuls it. [16] Now
the promises were made to Abraham and to his offspring; it does not
say, "And to offsprings," as of many; but it says, "And to your
offspring," that is, to one person, who is Christ. [17] My point is this:
the law, which came four hundred thirty years later, does not annul a
covenant previously ratified by God, so as to nullify the promise.
[18] For if the inheritance comes from the law, it no longer comes from
the promise; but God granted it to Abraham through the promise.

The Purpose of the Mosaic Law

[19] Why then the law? It was added because of transgressions, until the
offspring would come to whom the promise had been made; and it
was ordained through angels by a mediator. [20] Now a mediator
involves more than one party; but God is one.

[21] Is the law then opposed to the promises of God? Certainly not!
For if a law had been given that could make alive, then righteousness
would indeed come through the law. [22] But the scripture has imprisoned
all things under the power of sin, so that what was promised through
faith in Jesus Christ might be given to those who believe.

[23] Now before faith came, we were imprisoned and guarded
under the law until faith would be revealed. [24] Therefore the law was
our disciplinarian until Christ came, so that we might be justified by
faith. [25] But now that faith has come, we are no longer subject to a
disciplinarian, [26] for in Christ Jesus you are all children of God
through faith.

[27] As many of you as were baptized into Christ have clothed
yourselves with Christ. [28] There is no longer Jew or Greek, there is no
longer slave or free, there is no longer male and female; for all of you
are one in Christ Jesus. [29] And if you belong to Christ, then you are
Abraham's offspring, heirs according to the promise.

Childhood and Adulthood, Slavery and Freedom

1 My point is this: heirs, as long as they are minors, are no better than slaves, though they are the owners of all the property; 2 but they remain under guardians and trustees until the date set by the father. 3 So with us; while we were minors, we were enslaved to the elemental spirits of the world. 4 But when the fullness of time had come, God sent his Son, born of a woman, born under the law, 5 in order to redeem those who were under the law, so that we might receive adoption as children. 6 And because you are children, God has sent the Spirit of his Son into our hearts, crying, "Abba! Father!" 7 So you are no longer a slave but a child, and if a child then also an heir, through God.

8 Formerly, when you did not know God, you were enslaved to beings that by nature are not gods. 9 Now, however, that you have come to know God, or rather to be known by God, how can you turn back again to the weak and beggarly elemental spirits? How can you want to be enslaved to them again? 10 You are observing special days, and months, and seasons, and years. 11 I am afraid that my work for you may have been wasted.

A Reminder of Friendship

12 Friends, I beg you, become as I am, for I also have become as you are. You have done me no wrong.

13 You know that it was because of a physical infirmity that I first announced the gospel to you; 14 though my condition put you to the test, you did not scorn or despise me, but welcomed me as an angel of God, as Christ Jesus. 15 What has become of the goodwill you felt? For I testify that, had it been possible, you would have torn out your eyes and given them to me. 16 Have I now become your enemy by telling you the truth?

17 They make much of you, but for no good purpose; they want to exclude you, so that you may make much of them. 18 It is good to be made much of for a good purpose at all times, and not only when I am present with you.

19 My little children, for whom I am again in the pain of childbirth until Christ is formed in you, 20 I wish I were present with you now and could change my tone, for I am perplexed about you.

10 minutes
Choose questions according to your interest and time.

1 What picture of the Christian's relationship with God do you get by putting together Paul's statement in 4:6 with his statement in 2:20 (Week 3)?

2 In 4:10, is Paul forbidding Christians from having any holy days and feast days? How does the context of the statement help in answering this question?

3 Paul contrasts childhood with adulthood, slavery with freedom. What picture of adulthood and freedom does Paul give?

4 If you were one of the Galatians, how might you feel when you heard Paul's appeal in 4:12–20?

5 Paul reminds the Galatians of their friendship with him. What aspects of friendship between Paul and the Galatians can be seen in the letter so far, especially in 4:12–20?

A Guide to the Reading

If participants have not read this section already, read it aloud. Otherwise go on to "Questions for Application."

3:15–18. Once a person has made a will, no one else can alter it. Paul applies this principle to God's covenant with Abraham. Conveniently for Paul, the same Greek word means both "will" (as in 3:15) and "covenant" (as in 3:17). God's covenant with Abraham contained a promise of land to his offspring (Genesis 12:7). Once God made his promise, no one could add conditions to it. The Mosaic Law, which came on the scene long after the promise, consisted of requirements for the behavior of the Israelite people. But the fulfillment of the promise could not depend on whether or not the Israelites kept the Law. God's promise was irrevocable.

The heir of Abraham—Jesus—has now come and has inherited what was promised. Through Jesus, God makes his blessing available to all humankind. The blessing, however, has come in a form different than expected. The land that God promised symbolized something greater: the gift of the Holy Spirit (see 4:6; see also 3:14).

Paul emphasizes the difference between God's promise to Abraham and the Mosaic Law. The Law, Paul declares, was not connected to the promise; the Law was a holding action, a protective measure, for the period between God's making the promise and his fulfilling it. Paul's point, once more, is that there is no reason for the Galatians to embrace the Mosaic Law, which was a measure for an interim that has now ended.

For those of us who are not attracted by the idea of embracing the Mosaic Law, the aspect of Paul's argument that may hold the greatest interest is his insistence on the unconditional nature of God's dealings with Abraham. God made a promise to Abraham not because of anything Abraham had done but because of God's desire to bless him. For the same reason, God determined to keep his promise to Abraham despite anything Abraham or his descendants did or did not do. God's dealings with Abraham illustrate the free, unchanging kindness with which God acts toward all of us. God cares for us, even when we do not respond to him. God gives his grace to sinners. He offers to set us right, simply out of love.

3:19–25. Paul has emphasized that the Mosaic Law does not set people right with God or bring us God's life. What purpose, then, did the Law serve? It existed "because of transgressions," Paul explains. The Law curbed wrongdoing by helping people distinguish right from wrong, setting clear rules of behavior, and clarifying moral issues. A first-century Jewish writer described the Mosaic Law as a "fence" around the Jewish people, protecting them from the idolatry and immorality prevalent in surrounding cultures. Paul would probably have accepted that image. But he would have pointed out that while a wall is useful for guarding an orchard from marauders, it cannot make the trees grow (3:21).

Paul speaks of the world being "imprisoned" under sin (3:22). The picture is murky. Paul seems to view the world as a large territory dominated by dark powers ("the present evil age"— 1:4). Within this territory, the people of Israel were like a city walled about by the protecting Law of Moses. But the encircling wall of the Law not only guarded the inhabitants of the city; it also confined them (3:23).

Perhaps Paul's point is clearer in his comparisons of the Mosaic Law to a "disciplinarian" (3:24–25) and to "guardians" and "trustees" (4:2). The "disciplinarian" was a household slave who took charge of a boy until he reached manhood. Guardians and trustees cared for boys who lost their fathers before reaching adulthood, making legal and financial decisions for those in their care. The supervision provided by these adults was beneficial, but boys long to grow up and get free of such constraints.

The period of adulthood has now arrived with the coming of Jesus, Paul declares. So why would the Galatians want to submit to the Mosaic Law?

3:26–29. Paul's words on the equal sharing in Christ of Jews and non-Jews, slaves and free people, men and women, have profound implications for the life of the Church. But one implication is particularly important for Paul's argument: *all* who have become united with Christ receive the blessing that God promised to Abraham. Thus, yet again, gentile Christians have no need to become Jews.

Paul speaks of Christ as clothing we put on, perhaps the way an actor puts on clothes to play a particular part. But in the case of "playing Jesus," we are supposed to truly become like the character we are playing.

4:1–11. Paul's comparisons of the Mosaic Law to a disciplinarian, a trustee, or an administrator put the Law in a basically favorable light. All these are caretakers, who act on behalf of those in their charges. While the child may chafe at their supervision, it is not the kind of slavery that forces the child to labor for a master. For a time the boy cannot make decisions for himself. But, as he matures, he will grow out of this condition.

Now Paul puts the Mosaic Law in a less positive light. He speaks of being under the Law as an enslavement to "the elemental spirits of the world" (4:3). This is not a kindly supervision. Nor is it an authority that is outgrown; people need to be redeemed, or rescued, from this enslavement (4:5).

In what is surely one of the more obscure corners of his teaching, Paul even compares life under the Mosaic Law to life in pagan religion. He tells the gentile Christians that if they embrace the Mosaic Law they will be *returning* into the grip of the dark spiritual forces (the "weak and beggarly elemental spirits") that dominated their lives when they worshiped many gods and goddesses (4:9). Paul is working within a first-century view of the universe, in which hostile spiritual powers were thought to endanger and oppress human beings. He sees these dark forces as being capable of manipulating not only pagan religions but even the Law of Moses. Whatever the explanation of Paul's dim view of the Mosaic Law here, his point is clear enough: Jesus has set us free from all the powers of evil in the universe, no matter what they might be (4:4–5).

Jesus not only frees us from the forces of evil that would bind and destroy us. He shares with us his own intimate relationship with God. Paul sums up this gift in a single word in Aramaic, Jesus' everyday language: "Abba." This is the Aramaic word by which a child of any age spoke to his or her father. "Dad" is close to its meaning. "Dad" was Jesus' characteristic way of addressing God. By his Spirit living in us, it can become our way also.

4:12–20. Paul appeals to the Galatians as friends (4:12; compare 2 Corinthians 6:11–13). Friends have things in common. "Let us have Christ in common," Paul says to the Galatians. "Christ has carried me beyond distinctions between Jew and gentile. Let him carry you also beyond such distinctions."

The Galatians should remember the friendship they extended to Paul when he first came to them. Apparently he had some ailment (an eye disease?) that gave him an unpleasant appearance. Yet they overlooked his condition and received his words as a message from God. The Spirit must already have been at work among the Galatians, for how else could they have seen God in the "distressing disguise" of a visitor with an unpleasant affliction—to borrow a phrase from Mother Teresa of Calcutta, who spoke of glimpsing Christ in the distressing disguise of the poor.

But now the euphoria of conversion has faded away. Biblical scholar James Dunn suggests that as "so often in converts, the fading of the initial flush of enthusiasm resulted in an increasing dissatisfaction, which may have been a factor in their responding so positively to the other missionaries—in the hope that a further act of commitment would have brought again that 'first fine careless rapture.'"

Unfortunately, these other teachers have persuaded the Galatians that Paul is not their friend at all but their enemy (4:16), since he failed to instruct them in the necessity of following the Mosaic Law.

Paul's goal is that Jesus would become the center of the Galatians' lives (see 2:19–20) and of their local Christian communities (4:19). They are to become transformed into the image of Jesus (compare 2 Corinthians 3:18). But the process of change is proving to be longer and more difficult than Paul had expected, and Paul seems unsure why. Paul implies that he is so baffled by the Galatians that he has run out of arguments with which to persuade them. His bafflement is genuine enough, but he is not quite out of arguments, as you can see by glancing at the remainder of chapter 4.

Questions for Application

40 minutes
Choose questions according to your interest and time.

1 Jesus speaks of the necessity
of his followers becoming like
children (Mark 10:15). Paul
talks of the value of Christians
becoming like adults. How can
a person do both?

2 In relating to God, what
difference does it make to
know that God's love is
unconditional?

3 In what situations are laws
and rules important? In what
situations is there a problem
in relying on laws and rules?
What are laws and rules not
able to accomplish?

4 What kind of relationship with
God is suggested by addressing
him as "Dad"?

5 When have you been at a loss to know how to relate to a family member or friend? What did you do? What happened? What did you learn from this episode?

6 For personal reflection: Has there been a time in your life when you felt elated about your relationship with God? Has the feeling of spiritual euphoria gone away? What are the problems with trying to recapture a particular spiritual experience?

7 For personal reflection: Are you dealing with a situation where much hangs in the balance and there is no certainty that everything will work out right? What could you learn from Paul's way of handling his situation?

As we open ourselves to God's word, we not only grow as Christians: we actually expand our potential for growth. If any encounter with a good person is transforming and creative, how much more creative is an encounter with God, who is the source of all life, including our Christian life?

Eugene LaVerdiere, S.S.S., *The New Testament in the Life of the Church*

Approach to Prayer

15 minutes
Use this approach—or create your own!

◆ Pray Psalm 107 as a way of
thanking God for the freedom
he gives us in Christ. If everyone
in the group has the same trans-
lation of the Bible, pray it in
unison. Otherwise, let participants take turns reading
successive verses from their
translations.

Living Tradition

Spiritual Direction in a Nutshell

This section is a supplement for individual reading.

Columba Marmion was a Benedictine abbot and a renowned spiritual director in the late nineteenth and early twentieth centuries. In a very short letter to a friend he encapsulated his entire view of growth in the spiritual life.

I am happy to see that the Holy Spirit is making you understand that we have *all* in Jesus Christ. For this knowledge is the grain of mustard seed Our Lord speaks of, which to begin with is very small, then, on being cultivated, becomes a great tree.

Here, in a couple of words, is what I try to teach:

Jesus Christ is Infinite Holiness. . . . But he is not only holy in himself; he has been given to be *our* holiness . . . (1 Corinthians 1:30). He is our holiness:

As perfect *model.* . . .

And *as means of union with God.* In Jesus the divine nature and the human nature are united in one Person, and we are united with the Divinity in the measure of our union with the Sacred Humanity of Jesus. . . . It is by sanctifying grace that this union with God is brought about, and this grace is the work of the Blessed Trinity in us. . . .

The outpouring of this grace depends on Jesus Christ. He is the one who has merited it. He is the one who applies it to us. This grace tends to reproduce in us the features of Jesus Christ. And the more we lean upon him, the more abundant is this grace. . . .

All the graces that we receive work in the direction of making us, by grace of adoption, what Jesus is by nature—children of God. That is why this *same* Holy Spirit who was in Jesus, the principle of his whole human life, is given to us: "Because you are sons, God has sent the Spirit of his Son into our hearts, crying, 'Abba! Father!'" (Galatians 4:6, Revised Standard Version). It is this Holy Spirit who achieves in us the image of Jesus and fills us with his life (2 Corinthians 3:18).

There, in a few words, is all that I know.

Between Discussions

Two Puzzling Statements

We have met more than a few puzzling statements in Paul's letter to the Galatians (readers of Paul need to have a high tolerance for puzzlement!—see 2 Peter 3:15–16). In our most recent reading two statements, at least, raise question marks.

A passage in Genesis says that "The LORD appeared to Abram, and said, 'To your offspring I will give this land'" (Genesis 12:7). Paul makes a particular point of the fact that the word "offspring" here is singular. Paul writes: "Now the promises were made to Abraham and to his offspring; it does not say, 'And to offsprings,' as of many; but it says, 'And to your offspring,' that is, to one person, who is Christ" (3:16). Could Paul not have known that the Hebrew word here translated "offspring" (more literally "seed") is used as a collective, meaning not one individual but a group? Does Paul think that God's promise to Abraham was *not* to all his many descendants but only to *one?* Paul's argument seems highly artificial.

Clearly, Paul recognized that the term "offspring" here refers to many descendants. Abraham's offspring were proverbial for being "as numerous as the stars of heaven" and the grains of sand "on the seashore" (Genesis 22:17)—a rather obvious point with which Paul was well acquainted (Romans 4:16–18).

Nevertheless, it was a principle of interpretation in Paul's day that even minor features of the text, such as the fact that a word with collective meaning was singular in form, could have great significance. Using this principle, Paul draws a surprising conclusion from Genesis 12:7: God's promise to Abraham reaches its true, final fulfillment in one particular descendant: Jesus of Nazareth. In effect, Paul interprets Genesis 12:7 as a prophecy of the Messiah.

No matter how many descendants Abraham has in the people of Israel, and no matter how many of God's blessings they experience as they follow the Mosaic Law, God's promise to Abraham ultimately signified a supreme blessing that is inherited by *one* single descendant, Jesus. All God's blessings are for him; all God's blessing flow through him to the human race. Thus the gentile Galatians do not need to join Abraham's many descendants, the Jewish people, by becoming Jews. United by faith in Jesus

Christ, the *one* descendant of Abraham, the Galatians already have access to all God's blessings.

For ourselves, the message is that everything each of us needs for the life God has created us to live—the strength, wisdom, inspiration, encouragement, instruction, protection, resources, companionship, help—is available to us in Jesus.

Further on, Paul writes that the Mosaic Law "was ordained through angels by a mediator. Now a mediator involves more than one party; but God is one" (3:19–20). Most intriguing! More than a century ago a German scholar collected 400 proposed explanations of this statement. Here, briefly, is one explanation favored by some contemporary scholars.

On the basis of first-century speculations, rather than the text of the book of Exodus, Paul pictures the Law being conveyed to the people of Israel by angels. Two groups participated in the transaction. On one side were God's heavenly servants, the angels; on the other, God's earthly servants, the Israelite people. One person, Moses, acted as the representative of the people; correspondingly a single angel represented the angels. This angel is the "mediator" to whom Paul refers.

In this picture, God did not give the Law directly into the hand of Moses. Rather, God stood in the background and let the angels act for him. Thus the Mosaic Law came through a process of indirect communication between God and humans, in contrast to the promise to Abraham, which God gave directly. The promise to Abraham, then, has priority over the Law given to Israel, because the promise came more directly from God.

Since the Galatians are already descendants of Abraham through Jesus, they have entered into the most direct relationship possible with God. Hence, yet again, there is no reason for them to embrace the Mosaic Law.

We may tire of Paul's repeated insistence on this point, but we must admire his creativity in finding so many ways to make his case. Paul is at a loss to understand why the Galatians are attracted to the Mosaic Law (see 3:1; 4:20). So perhaps he is shooting in the dark, using every argument he can think of, hoping that at least one strikes home.

The Power of Love

Questions to Begin

15 minutes
Use a question or two to get warmed up for the reading.

1   What are you looking forward to this month? this year?

2   When have you made a good start but failed to carry through to a successful conclusion?

5 minutes
Read the passage aloud. Let individuals take turns reading paragraphs.

What's Happened

After last week's reading, Paul makes one final attempt to convince the Galatian Christians that following the Mosaic Law will not bring them any benefits they do not already enjoy in Christ. His argument (4:21–31) is based on a comparison of two of Abraham's wives and their sons. Abraham's wife, Sarah, bore Isaac; earlier, her slave, Hagar, bore Abraham a son named Ishmael. In these events, Paul believes, God gave a symbolic foreshadowing of the situation that Jesus has brought about through his death, resurrection, and gift of his Spirit to his followers. The two mothers and their sons symbolize two communities, one characterized by freedom, the other by slavery. Isaac, the son of the free woman, Sarah, symbolizes those who believe in Jesus and experience freedom from the powers of evil at work in the world and within themselves. Ishmael, born of a slave woman, symbolizes those who are bound to the Mosaic Law, which does not bring freedom from the deepest evils that afflict humankind.

The Reading: Galatians 5:1–24

Stand Tall

¹ For freedom Christ has set us free. Stand firm, therefore, and do not submit again to a yoke of slavery.

² Listen! I, Paul, am telling you that if you let yourselves be circumcised, Christ will be of no benefit to you. ³ Once again I testify to every man who lets himself be circumcised that he is obliged to obey the entire law. ⁴ You who want to be justified by the law have cut yourselves off from Christ; you have fallen away from grace. ⁵ For through the Spirit, by faith, we eagerly wait for the hope of righteousness. ⁶ For in Christ Jesus neither circumcision nor uncircumcision counts for anything; the only thing that counts is faith working through love.

Get Back on Track

7 You were running well; who prevented you from obeying the truth?
8 Such persuasion does not come from the one who calls you. 9 A
little yeast leavens the whole batch of dough. 10 I am confident about
you in the Lord that you will not think otherwise. But whoever it is
that is confusing you will pay the penalty. 11 But my friends, why am I
still being persecuted if I am still preaching circumcision? In that case
the offense of the cross has been removed. 12 I wish those who
unsettle you would castrate themselves!

Stay Focused

13 For you were called to freedom, brothers and sisters; only do not
use your freedom as an opportunity for self-indulgence,a but through
love become slaves to one another. 14 For the whole law is summed
up in a single commandment, "You shall love your neighbor as
yourself." 15 If, however, you bite and devour one another, take care
that you are not consumed by one another.

Keep in Step with the Spirit

16 Live by the Spirit, I say, and do not gratify the desires of the flesh.
17 For what the flesh desires is opposed to the Spirit, and what the
Spirit desires is opposed to the flesh; for these are opposed to each
other, to prevent you from doing what you want. 18 But if you are led
by the Spirit, you are not subject to the law.

19 Now the works of the flesh are obvious: fornication,
impurity, licentiousness, 20 idolatry, sorcery, enmities, strife, jealousy,
anger, quarrels, dissensions, factions, 21 envy, drunkenness, carousing,
and things like these. I am warning you, as I warned you before: those
who do such things will not inherit the kingdom of God.

22 By contrast, the fruit of the Spirit is love, joy, peace,
patience, kindness, generosity, faithfulness, 23 gentleness, and self-
control. There is no law against such things. 24 And those who belong
to Christ Jesus have crucified the flesh with its passions and desires.

a Greek *the flesh*

Questions for Careful Reading

10 minutes
Choose questions according to your interest and time.

1 How many reasons does Paul give in 5:2–6 for Christians not to follow the Mosaic Law?

2 Compare 5:1 with 5:13. Is Paul talking about the same kind of freedom in both verses? Is he talking about the same kind of slavery in both verses?

3 If you were to adapt 5:6 as a slogan for your parish or Christian group, what would you substitute for "circumcision" and "uncircumcision"?

4 Freedom is a major effect of the Spirit (5:1), so why doesn't Paul include it among the fruit of the Spirit (5:22–23)?

5 Compare Paul's confidence about the Galatians in 5:10 with his earlier anxiety (1:6; 3:1–4; 4:9–11, 15–16, 19–20; 5:4). How would you explain the differences?

A Guide to the Reading

If participants have not read this section already, read it aloud. Otherwise go on to "Questions for Application."

5:1–6. Paul goes for broke in this final appeal to his Galatian converts. All along, he has been trying to convince them that they do not need to follow the Mosaic Law. But this is the first time Paul says explicitly that the men do not need to be circumcised— circumcision being the sign that a man, and the household linked to him, accepts the Mosaic Law. If they do get circumcised, Paul declares, they will be cut off from Christ, for they will implicitly be denying that Jesus' death and resurrection is enough to set them right. To think that Christ is insufficient to save us is to deny who Christ is and what he has done.

Paul speaks of Christians being "in Christ" (5:6) and shows that union with Christ is not a static condition but a source of tremendous energy. Faith takes hold of God's grace and turns outward in concern for others. Paul implies that faith that does not express itself in love is not real (an implication that another New Testament writer makes explicit: see James 2:17–18). "In Paul's view," writes Hans Dieter Betz, "the Christian is not merely an individual who has belief in Jesus Christ, but by being such a believer, he has become a channel for the divine power"—the power of love.

5:7–12. Throughout the letter, Paul has emphasized that Jesus, crucified and risen, is the only one with the power to overcome sin and evil. Yet this emphasis does not lead Paul to a passive view of Christian life. Real faith *works:* it cooperates with the Spirit working within us. Paul's view of Christian living is vigorous and robust. Here he compares Christian life to running (5:7)—an activity that takes great effort and determination.

Paul's wish that those who advocate circumcision would cut off more than their foreskins is a bit of coarse humor (5:12)— and an indication of how exasperated he is with the situation in Galatia.

5:13–24. Paul describes a struggle between "the flesh" and "the Spirit." (The Greek word translated "self-indulgence" in 5:13 is the same word translated "the flesh" in 5:16, 17, 19, 24.) The flesh is not the material side of our nature, in contrast to our mind or soul. Rather, it is our weakness in the face of pressures and inducements to sin. Sins of the flesh can involve not just our bodies but any part of our human makeup, as can be seen from the list of effects of the flesh, many of which have to do with thinking and speaking, rather than with sensual desires ("enmities, strife, jealousy, anger, quarrels, dissensions, factions, envy"—5:20–21).

But Paul regards the flesh not only as our weakness in the face of temptations but as a kind of superhuman power that seeks to establish a base of operations in our lives. In Paul's mind, the flesh is like the "elemental spirits" of the world—an evil force at work in "the present evil age." But opposing the flesh is the Holy Spirit, who, being God, is infinitely more powerful than the flesh.

Like God's Son, God's Spirit has arrived on the human scene to overturn the powers of evil. With the coming of the Spirit to Christians, God has launched a war of liberation in the world. Now the Spirit and the flesh are locked in combat. As Christians, we are not a mere battlefield where these two forces struggle against each other. We have been recruited to cooperate with the Spirit, to join in the Spirit's efforts to free the world from the grip of evil.

Paul's statement about our being prevented from doing what we want (5:17) seems to mean that we cannot weave back and forth between the flesh and the Spirit, sometimes aligning ourselves with one and sometimes with the other. There's a war on! We are participants in the end-times conflict between the Spirit of God and the powers of evil that oppose God's reign. We must choose which side we are on and take a stand. Our difficulty, of course, is that we ourselves are divided. Both the flesh and the Spirit have a foothold in us. The battle is a battle within ourselves. Every day, we must choose which part of ourselves we will side with.

To some extent, Paul's exhortation (5:13–14) has a warning tone. Freedom has its dangers. Released by Christ from the power of sin—and without the discipline of the Mosaic Law— we must use our freedom responsibly. We are challenged to use our freedom to serve our neighbors (5:13). Paul goes so far as to call this love a form of slavery. Although love is always voluntary, it does not always bubble spontaneously to the surface. When circumstances become difficult and loving sentiments fade away, true love carries on with commitment—which is a kind of slavery, as well as the deepest kind of freedom.

Yet, more than warning, Paul's fundamental goal in this section is to encourage. He reassures the Galatians about where they stand in the battle between good and evil. The Galatians may have needed encouragement. While it is possible that they were sinning freely without any concern for God, it is more likely that, like many Christians today, they were painfully aware of their sins. Quite possibly they were looking for a remedy. In all likelihood, the other teachers were offering one. God's remedy for sin, they were telling the Galatians, is the Mosaic Law. "The Law will give you the guidance and discipline you need to overcome the impulsive, insistent desires of the flesh that lead you into sin."

In effect, Paul responds, "I am well aware of the sins of the flesh (5:19–21). And I am convinced that the flesh is too big a power to be overcome by the Mosaic Law. The only complete and total remedy for the power of the flesh is the Holy Spirit—the Spirit you have already received."

In 5:16, what seems like a command—"Live by the Spirit . . . and do not gratify the desires of the flesh"—might better be translated as an assurance: If you walk by the Spirit, you *will not* satisfy the desires of the flesh. If you orient your life to the Holy Spirit, Paul implies, sinful tendencies will eventually get neutralized, squeezed out, and replaced. Paul does not deny that developing good habits, character training, self-discipline, and so on, are important factors in living a good life and becoming a good person. But he underlines the essential factors: being attentive to the presence and promptings of the Spirit, relying on the Spirit's power, and cooperating with the Spirit's initiatives. Of course, our efforts to do good play a key part; our "self-control" is part of the process of maturing (5:23). But self-control is not the engine of our transformation. It is, rather, an effect of the Spirit living within us.

The Spirit works from within us. Notice Paul's reference to "what the Spirit desires" (5:17). The Spirit has come into our minds and hearts to plant his desires in us—new desires, desires for God's kingdom—which ultimately will replace all our lesser, selfish desires. As the Spirit carries out his mysterious work in us, what brings us joy changes, and our capacity for joy grows (notice "joy" among "the fruit of the Spirit"—5:22). We come to desire God and the extension of his love to all his creation—and we have the joy of knowing that this desire will ultimately be fulfilled.

"The whole law is summed up in a single commandment, 'You shall love your neighbor as yourself,'" Paul declares (5:14). Paul may well be referring to Jesus' death on the cross. By his death out of love for us (2:20), Jesus brought the whole Mosaic Law to perfection by putting into practice its central purpose: love of neighbor. Love of neighbor, God's original purpose for the Law, was not revealed in all its brilliance and beauty until Jesus gave us his life to redeem us from the powers of sin and evil and death. Thus Paul's message is simple: To overcome the flesh, live in the Spirit. And to know what it means to live in the Spirit, look at Jesus' example of self-giving love.

"Love," then, as "the fruit of the Spirit" (5:22) is probably not just the first on the list but the quality that embraces every aspect of the fruit of the Spirit. Love is *the* fruit of the Spirit, the outward manifestation of a divine power within Christ's followers, the inner force that seeks to express itself in our lives as powerfully as vegetation springing up at winter's end, poking up in every square inch of soil, roots thrusting stones aside, and flowers blooming in all the crevices in the rocks.

Questions for Application

40 minutes
Choose questions according to your interest and time.

1 In Paul's view, what does Jesus bring us freedom from? What does he bring us freedom for?

2 How do the works of the flesh affect a family, a parish, a civic community? what about the fruit of the Spirit?

3 One commentator remarks that Paul's approach to overcoming the flesh—being led by the Spirit, following the Spirit—is "disarmingly simple, and perhaps naive." What do you think?

4 Through the Spirit, Christ sets us free and brings us to maturity. But he uses agents and instruments. What are some of them? Who and what have been some of the most important in your life?

5 When have you experienced the Spirit as the power of love within you? What have you learned from this experience? Where could you apply this lesson in your life today?

6 When have you experienced the Spirit helping you to change in ways that you could not have thought would be possible? How has this affected your relationship with God?

7 What step could you take to allow the Holy Spirit to fill more of your life?

8 For personal reflection: Which of the fruit of the Spirit (5:22–23) do you find it most difficult to produce? Have you asked the Spirit to help you grow in this area of your life?

One doesn't have to be a literary critic to read a novel, and one doesn't have to be a biblical scholar to read Scripture. One can get a great deal at any level but should always be open to further growth and development.

Clarence and Edith Roberts, *Sharing of Scripture*

Approach to Prayer

15 minutes
Use this approach—or create your own!

◆ Let one participant read John 15:1–17 aloud. Allow for silent reflection. Invite participants who wish to, to offer brief prayers. Close with an Our Father.

Saints in the Making

Discovering Joy

This section is a supplement for individual reading.

A nineteenth-century Protestant missionary who faced great obstacles in China, J. Hudson Taylor went through a period of darkness in his relationship with God. In a letter, he described his experience to his sister in England:

I prayed, agonized, fasted, strove, made resolutions, read the Word more diligently, sought more time for meditation—but all without avail. Every day, almost every hour, the consciousness of sin oppressed me. . . . I would begin the day with prayer, determined not to take my eye off him for a moment, but pressure of duties, sometimes very trying, and constant interruptions apt to be so wearing, caused me to forget him. Then one's nerves get so fretted in this climate that temptations to irritability, hard thoughts and sometimes unkind words are all the more difficult to control. Each day brought its register of sin and failure. . . . All the time I felt assured that there was in Christ all I needed, but the practical question was—how to get it out. . . .

[But] as I thought of the vine and the branches, what light the blessed Spirit poured direct into my soul! . . . How great seemed my mistake in wishing to get the sap, the fullness out of him! . . . The vine is not the root merely, but all—root, stem, branches, twigs, leaves, flowers, fruit. And Jesus is not that alone—he is soil and sunshine, air and showers, and ten thousand times more than we have ever dreamed, wished for or needed. . . .

I am no longer anxious about anything, as I realize this; for he, I know, is able to carry out his will, and his will is mine. It makes no matter where he places me, or how. That is rather for him to consider than for me; for in the easiest position he must give me his grace, and in the most difficult his grace is sufficient. . . .

And since Christ has thus dwelt in my heart by faith, how happy I have been! I wish I could tell you about it, instead of writing. I am no better than before. . . . But I am dead and buried with Christ—ay, and risen too!—And now Christ lives in me, and "the life that I now live in the flesh, I live by the faith of the Son of God, who loved me and gave himself for me."

Making It Practical

Questions to Begin

15 minutes
Use a question or two to get warmed up for the reading.

1 Describe an act of kindness to you that made a lasting impression on you.

2 In school or in any other setting, who has been your favorite teacher? Why?

5 minutes
Read the passage aloud. Let individuals take turns reading paragraphs.

The Reading: Galatians 5:22–6:18

Encouragements, Reminders, Warnings

22 . . . the fruit of the Spirit is love, joy, peace, patience, kindness, generosity, faithfulness, 23 gentleness, and self-control. There is no law against such things. 24 And those who belong to Christ Jesus have crucified the flesh with its passions and desires.

25 If we live by the Spirit, let us also be guided by the Spirit.

26 Let us not become conceited, competing against one another, envying one another.

1 My friends, if anyone is detected in a transgression, you who have received the Spirit should restore such a one in a spirit of gentleness.

Take care that you yourselves are not tempted.

2 Bear one another's burdens, and in this way you will fulfill the law of Christ.

3 For if those who are nothing think they are something, they deceive themselves. 4 All must test their own work; then that work, rather than their neighbor's work, will become a cause for pride. 5 For all must carry their own loads.

6 Those who are taught the word must share in all good things with their teacher.

7 Do not be deceived; God is not mocked, for you reap whatever you sow. 8 If you sow to your own flesh, you will reap corruption from the flesh; but if you sow to the Spirit, you will reap eternal life from the Spirit. 9 So let us not grow weary in doing what is right, for we will reap at harvest time, if we do not give up. 10 So then, whenever we have an opportunity, let us work for the good of all, and especially for those of the family of faith.

A Personal Word from the Apostle

11 See what large letters I make when I am writing in my own hand!

12 It is those who want to make a good showing in the flesh that try to compel you to be circumcised—only that they may not be persecuted for the cross of Christ. 13 Even the circumcised do not themselves obey the law, but they want you to be circumcised so that they may boast about your flesh. 14 May I never boast of anything

except the cross of our Lord Jesus Christ, by which the world has been crucified to me, and I to the world. 15 For neither circumcision nor uncircumcision is anything; but a new creation is everything! 16 As for those who will follow this rule—peace be upon them, and mercy, and upon the Israel of God.

17 From now on, let no one make trouble for me; for I carry the marks of Jesus branded on my body.

Ending on a Positive Note

18 May the grace of our Lord Jesus Christ be with your spirit, brothers and sisters. Amen.

10 minutes
Choose questions according to your interest and time.

1 How are Paul's instructions in 5:25–6:10 related to the particular fruit-of-the-Spirit qualities he lists in 5:22–23?

2 Paul has been insisting that the Law of Moses does not set people right with God and give them life. In what ways are his instructions in 5:25–6:10 like a law? In what ways are they different from a law?

3 Compare 6:1 with 2:14. Did Paul take his own advice?

4 Compare 6:2 with 6:5. Does Paul contradict himself?

5 What does 6:11 imply about how Paul has been writing the letter before this point?

A Guide to the Reading

If participants have not read this section already, read it aloud. Otherwise go on to "Questions for Application."

5:22–6:10. Paul has spoken about the fruit of the Spirit in general terms. But he is not satisfied with his discussion until he makes it practical. What kinds of things does the Spirit lead us to do?

One activity very much in keeping with the Spirit is sober self-knowledge. Truly spiritual people do not let their spiritual experiences waft them up to an exalted view of their spiritual maturity ("let us not become conceited"—5:26). When they offer advice or criticism, they maintain an awareness of their own tendencies to sin (6:1; compare Matthew 7:1–5). They keep a sober estimate of their strengths and weaknesses (6:3). Realism about oneself is rarely thought of as a gift of the Spirit, but from Paul's exhortations it stands out as one of the most important effects of the Spirit's activity in us. It is also a key to continuing to experience the action of the Spirit. An awareness of our weaknesses helps us to depend on the Spirit.

Realism about ourselves, in Paul's view, includes recognizing our achievements. There is a certain kind of pride we can take in work done well according to God's measurements (6:4). But this is different from the kind of pride that asserts that our work is better than someone else's (6:4) and seeks to demonstrate our superiority over others (5:26). The Spirit is not interested in helping us outshine other people but in helping us perceive their needs in order to help them along the road of life (6:1–2, 9–10).

6:11–17. Becoming people who truly live according to the "law of Christ" (6:2) is no easy process, even with the help of the Spirit. The "flesh"—our tendency to live for ourselves, to live purely on the level of our own human needs and desires— constantly drags us in the wrong direction. Yet God offers us freedom. And, paradoxically, the divine power that brings us freedom comes through Jesus' human weakness, indeed through the utter weakness of his death on a cross.

Paul does not provide a complete explanation of his thinking on this subject. But he says enough to enable us to see that Jesus' death is an enduring reality that somehow lies open to us. We may enter into Jesus' death and share in it. By sharing in

Jesus' literal, physical death on the cross, we experience a death to the powers of evil that entangle us, both within ourselves and in the world around us. In some fundamental way, our connection to these powers of evil dies; their power over us is broken.

Paul spoke of this mysterious sharing in Jesus' death earlier when he discussed the breakup of his relationship with the Mosaic Law: "Through the law I died to the law, so that I might live to God. I have been crucified with Christ; and it is no longer I who live, but it is Christ who lives in me. And the life I now live in the flesh I live by faith in the Son of God, who loved me and gave himself for me" (2:19–20). In our present reading, Paul speaks of sharing in Jesus' death as the means by which we break our tie to the flesh: "Those who belong to Christ Jesus have crucified the flesh with its passions and desires" (5:24). Finally, in his concluding remarks, Paul writes, "May I never boast of anything except the cross of our Lord Jesus Christ, by which the world has been crucified to me, and I to the world" (6:14). By "the world" Paul means the values, patterns, and spiritual powers that oppose God in human society. Paul's allegiance and submission to them has been terminated by his entering into Jesus' death, dying to the self-directed person he was, and beginning a new life in union with Jesus.

6:18. Paul speaks of our sharing in Jesus' death as both a decisive, once-and-for-all event and as a continuing state of affairs. When we became Christians, we died with Christ to the flesh and the world—and we are still dying today. Each day brings new opportunities to die with Jesus to our own selfishness and the world's distorted values and to keep in step with the Spirit (5:25). No matter how great the difficulties we may face, such a life is a great gift, and is lived only by God's gift. Thus Paul closes his letter with a reminder of God's "grace."

Questions for Application

40 minutes
Choose questions according to your interest and time.

1 Pick one of the fruit of the Spirit (5:22–23), and identify someone you have known who exemplifies that quality. How was that quality expressed in their life? How did that quality develop in them? What can you learn from their experience about growing in that quality?

2 What have you learned about being guided by the Holy Spirit (5:25)? How can a person grow in being guided by the Spirit?

3 Reread 6:2. Think of a person you know who is burdened in a special way. What could you do to share that person's burden?

4 What criteria should a person use to evaluate their life ("all must test their own work"— 6:4)?

5 What examples can you suggest to show what it means to die to the world (6:14)?

6 For personal reflection: Reread 6:3–4. In what ways do you tend to think too highly or too poorly of yourself? What does this reading, or anything else that Paul has said in Galatians, suggest about how you should evaluate yourself?

Some medicines work against some kinds of sickness, but not against them all. But the word of God works against every kind of spiritual sickness.

Blessed Humbert of Romans, *Treatise on the Formation of Preachers*

Approach to Prayer

15 minutes
Use this approach—or create your own!

♦ Begin with an Our Father. Allow an opportunity for participants to mention briefly those they know who are burdened in some way. Then pray Psalm 25 on behalf of all the people who have been mentioned. End with a Glory to the Father.

Saints in the Making

Bear one another's burdens—Galatians 6:2

This section is a supplement for individual reading.

S atoko Kitahara came of age in difficult times. She was twelve years old in 1941, when Japan went to war against the United States. At fifteen she was working to the point of exhaustion at a Tokyo airplane factory. By the time Japan surrendered, in August 1945, she had fallen seriously ill with tuberculosis.

Satoko, however, came from a wealthy family. She had been raised in comfort and received an excellent education. When the war ended, she was able to convalesce and begin studies at a university.

Few Japanese were so fortunate. Most scrambled to recover from the war. Some were left totally destitute. In the normal course of events, Satoko would never have had any contact with the postwar underclass. But her life did not follow a normal course. A chance visit to a Catholic church led to her investigate Christianity and eventually to be baptized. Then, through a Franciscan brother named Zeno, she met a group of squatters who called themselves the Ant People. They eked out a miserable existence by collecting and selling trash. After meeting the Ant People, Satoko said, "How utterly blind I have been. I am ashamed."

Zeno asked Satoko to do some activities with the children. Soon she was not only visiting them but was bringing them home to practice singing around her piano. After each visit, her mother would carefully disinfect her clothes.

The Ant People appreciated Satoko's efforts but considered her a mere do-gooder. As Satoko got to know them, however, she wanted to share their life. She got a cart and went out collecting trash with them. People were astonished. Some thought she was crazy.

After a while, her work with the Ant People wore her out, and the tuberculosis returned. Soon she seemed close to death. Her doctor suggested that she would be happier among her friends, so her parents helped her move into Ant Town. For a while she could do some light work. When that became impossible, she spent her time praying for her Ant Town friends—especially that the city would sell them some land where they could make a new start. The agreement from the city came at about the same time that Satoko died, at the age of twenty-eight.

Suggestions for Bible Discussion Groups

Like a camping trip, a Bible discussion group works best if you agree on where you're going and how you intend to get there. Many groups use their first meeting to talk over such questions. Here is a checklist of issues, with bits of advice from people who have experience in Bible discussions. (A planning discussion will go more smoothly if the leaders have thought through the following issues beforehand.)

Agree on your purpose. Are you getting together to gain wisdom and direction for your lives? to finally get acquainted with the Bible? to support one another in following Christ? to encourage those who are exploring—or reexploring—the Church? for other reasons?

Agree on attitudes. For example: "We're all beginners here." "We're here to help one another understand and respond to God's word." "We're not here to offer counseling or direction to each other." "We want to read Scripture prayerfully." What do *you* wish to emphasize? Make it explicit!

Agree on ground rules. Barbara J. Fleischer, in her useful book *Facilitating for Growth,* recommends that a group clearly state its approach to the following:

- *Preparation.* Do we agree to read the material and prepare the answers to the questions before each meeting?
- *Attendance.* What kind of priority will we give to our meetings?
- *Self-revelation.* Are we willing to help the others in the group gradually get to know us—our weaknesses as well as our strengths, our needs as well as our gifts?
- *Listening.* Will we commit ourselves to listen to one another?
- *Confidentiality.* Will we keep everything that is shared *with* the group *in* the group?
- *Discretion.* Will we refrain from sharing about the faults and sins of people who are not in the group?
- *Encouragement and support.* Will we give as well as receive?
- *Participation.* Will we give each person the time and opportunity to make a contribution?

You could probably take a pen and draw a circle around *listening* and *confidentiality.* Those two points are especially important.

The following items could be added to Fleischer's list:

♦ *Relationship with parish.* Is our group part of the adult faith-formation program? independent but operating with the express approval of the pastor? not a parish-based group?

♦ *New members.* Will we let new members join us once we have begun the six weeks of discussions?

Agree on housekeeping.

♦ *When will we meet?*

♦ *How often will we meet?* Meeting weekly or every other week is best if you can manage it. William Riley remarks, "Meetings once a month are too distant from each other for the threads of the last session not to be lost" *(The Bible Study Group: An Owner's Manual).*

♦ *How long will meetings run?*

♦ *Where will we meet?*

♦ *Is any setup needed?* Christine Dodd writes that "the problem with meeting in a place like a church hall is that it can be very soul-destroying" given the cold, impersonal feel of many church facilities. If you have to meet in a church facility, Dodd recommends doing something to make the area homey *(Making Scripture Work).*

♦ *Who will host the meetings?* Leaders and hosts are not necessarily the same people.

♦ *Will we have refreshments?* Who will provide them? Don Cousins and Judson Poling make this recommendation: "Serve refreshments if you like, but save snacks and other foods for the end of the meeting to minimize distractions" *(Leader's Guide 1).*

♦ *What about child care?* Most experienced leaders of Bible discussion groups discourage bringing infants or other children to adult Bible discussions.

Agree on leadership. You need someone to facilitate—to keep the discussion on track, to see that everyone has a chance to speak, to help the group stay on schedule. Rena Duff, editor of the newsletter *Sharing God's Word Today,* recommends having two or three people take turns leading the discussions.

It's okay if the leader is not an expert on the Bible. You have this booklet, and if questions come up that no one can answer, you can delegate a participant to do a little research between meetings. Perhaps someone on the pastoral staff of your parish could offer advice. Or help may be available from your diocesan catechetical office or a local Catholic institution of higher learning.

It's important for the leader to set an example of listening, to draw out the quieter members (and occasionally restrain the more vocal ones), to move the group on when it gets stuck, to remind the members of their agreements, and to summarize what the group is accomplishing.

Bible discussion is an opportunity to experience the fulfillment of Jesus' promise "Where two or three are gathered in my name, I am there among them" (Matthew 18:20). Put your discussion group in Jesus' hands. Pray for the guidance of the Spirit. And have a great time exploring God's word together!

Suggestions for Individuals

You can use this booklet just as well for individual study as for group discussion. While discussing the Bible with other people can be a rich experience, there are advantages to reading on your own. For example:

♦ You can focus on the points that interest you most.

♦ You can go at your own pace.

♦ You can be completely relaxed and unashamedly honest in your answers to all the questions, since you don't have to share them with anyone!

My suggestions for using this booklet on your own are these:

♦ Don't skip the Questions to Begin. The questions can help you as an individual reader warm up to the topic of the reading.

♦ Take your time on the Questions for Careful Reading and Questions for Application. While a group will probably not have enough time to work on all the questions, you can allow yourself the time to consider all of them if you are using the booklet by yourself.

♦ After reading the Guide to the Reading, go back and reread the Scripture text before answering the Questions for Application.

♦ Take the time to look up all the parenthetical Scripture references in the introduction, the Guides to the Readings, and the other material.

♦ Since you control the pace, give yourself plenty of opportunities to reflect on the meaning of Galatians for you. Let your reading be an opportunity for these words to become God's words to you.

Bibles

The following editions of the Bible contain the full set of biblical books recognized by the Catholic Church, along with a great deal of useful explanatory material:

- ◆ The Catholic Study Bible (Oxford University Press), which uses the text of the New American Bible
- ◆ The Catholic Bible: Personal Study Edition (Oxford University Press), which also uses the text of the New American Bible
- ◆ The New Jerusalem Bible, the regular (not the reader's) edition (Doubleday)

Books

- ◆ James D. G. Dunn, *The Epistle to the Galatians,* Black's New Testament Commentaries, vol. 9 (Peabody, Mass.: Hendrickson Publishers, 1993).
- ◆ Frank J. Matera, *Galatians,* Sacra Pagina Series, vol. 9 (Collegeville, Minn.: Liturgical Press, 1992).

How has Scripture had an impact on your life? Was this booklet helpful to you in your study of the Bible? Please send comments, suggestions, and personal experiences to Kevin Perrotta, General Editor, Trade Editorial Department, Loyola Press, 3441 N. Ashland Ave., Chicago, IL 60657.